Snobol Programr
for the Humanities

Snobol Programming for the Humanities

SUSAN HOCKEY

CLARENDON PRESS · OXFORD
1985

Oxford University Press, Walton Street, Oxford OX2 6DP
Oxford New York Toronto
Delhi Bombay Calcutta Madras Karachi
Kuala Lumpur Singapore Hong Kong Tokyo
Nairobi Dar es Salaam Cape Town
Melbourne Auckland
and associated companies in
Beirut Berlin Ibadan Nicosia

Oxford is a trade mark of Oxford University Press

Published in the United States
by Oxford University Press, New York

British Library Cataloguing in Publication Data
Hockey, Susan M.
SNOBOL programming for the humanities.
1. Humanities—Data processing
I. Title
001.3'028'54   AZ105
ISBN 0–19–824675–7
ISBN 0–19–824676–5 Pbk

Library of Congress Cataloging in Publication Data
Hockey, Susan M.
Snobol programming for the humanities.
Bibliography: p.
Includes index.
1. SNOBOL (Computer program language)
2. Humanities—Data processing.
I. Title
QA76.73.S6H63   1985   005.13'3   85–15422
ISBN 0–19–824675–7
ISBN 0–19–824676–5 (pbk.)

Typeset on a Monotype Lasercomp
at Oxford University Computing Service
Printed in Great Britain
at the University Press, Oxford
by David Stanford
Printer to the University

Preface

SNOBOL is different from most computer programming languages. Computers evolved from mathematical studies, and most programming languages were designed to solve mathematical or scientific problems or to process numeric data. SNOBOL, on the other hand, was written to handle text rather than numbers and is therefore particularly suitable for studies in the humanities.

This book is an introduction to computer programming using SNOBOL. It is intended for the complete beginner with no previous computing experience. It is written very much with the humanities scholar in mind and no mathematical knowledge is necessary.

As well as those who wish to learn SNOBOL for a specific project, it is hoped that this book will also interest those who wish to learn to program for its own sake. For those without a scientific background SNOBOL offers an opportunity to gain an insight into computer programming without having to grapple with unfamiliar mathematical concepts.

SNOBOL originated in the early 1960s. The early versions (SNOBOL1, SNOBOL2 and SNOBOL3) rapidly became obsolete. The subject of this book is SNOBOL4, which soon became the normal version and is usually now called simply SNOBOL. One chapter of the book deals with SPITBOL, a version of SNOBOL which has some additional features and runs faster. The book also deals with the recent development of SNOBOL and SPITBOL for use on the IBM Personal Computer and other microcomputers.

Contents

1 Getting Started

1.1 Why Learn Snobol

SNOBOL is a computer language which was designed specifically for handling text rather than numbers. It is particularly suitable for humanities applications, both for text analysis and for handling data from research in history, archaeology or music. No mathematical knowledge is necessary for programming in SNOBOL and this book is intended to be understood by those who have had no previous experience of computer programming.

SNOBOL is an acronym for StriNg Oriented SymBOlic Language. The word *string* is a computer term which means a sequence of characters such as a word or a line of text.

1.2 Preparing a Program

A program is a sequence of instructions to be performed by the computer. The program is presented to the computer in a coded or symbolic form using statements in a specific programming language such as SNOBOL.

1.2.1 Algorithms

Before a program can be written, the problem which it is to solve must be broken down into a series of logical steps so that the procedure to be followed by the program can be clearly defined. This process is called constructing an algorithm.

1.2.2 A Simple Program

Suppose that we wanted to write a program to count the number of times that the name WILLIAM occurs in a text. The algorithm would be something like

1. Get a line of data.
2. Is WILLIAM in the line?
3. If so, count it and go back to stage 2, otherwise go to stage 1.
4. When all instances of WILLIAM in one line have been dealt with, go to stage 1.

We have to allow for more than one occurrence of WILLIAM within a line. Stages 2 and 3 are repeated for each occurrence of WILLIAM within a line. Stage 1 is repeated for each line. When all the data has been dealt with, the last stage is to print the total.

A SNOBOL program for the algorithm given above could be

```
        &ANCHOR = 0
MORE    LINE = INPUT              :F(PRINT)
AGAIN   LINE 'WILLIAM' =          :F(MORE)
        COUNT = COUNT + 1         :(AGAIN)
PRINT   OUTPUT = 'NUMBER OF OCCURRENCES OF "WILLIAM" IS ' COUNT
END
```

The program gets hold of each line of its data in turn and looks for WILLIAM within it. If WILLIAM is found, the number 1 is added to the running total, the count. &ANCHOR = 0 makes sure that WILLIAM is found anywhere in a line, not just at the beginning, and the program statement which looks for WILLIAM handles multiple occurrences within a line. When all the lines of data have been dealt with, a message is printed giving the total.

This is a simple program using only capital letters in its data, but it does illustrate the kind of procedure which must be followed. The reader will have encountered almost all the SNOBOL syntax required for this program by the end of this chapter.

1.2.3   Program Syntax

The syntax of the program must conform to the rules for the particular programming language. Otherwise the computer will not be able to understand it and will respond with error messages when the program is presented to it.

1.2.4   Execution of the Program

Even if the syntax of the program is correct, the execution may not succeed if there are errors in the logical sequence of instructions. If this happens, the program usually terminates abruptly, giving one or more error messages. It is also possible to write a program which terminates correctly but produces incorrect answers. Once a program works, it may be run many times on different data.

1.3   Variables

Like most programming languages, SNOBOL uses *variables* to hold information. A program can contain many variables, each of which is an object or item which is required for the operation of the program. In the example program above, LINE and COUNT are variables. A variable can be thought of as a box which has both a name and some contents. It can contain either characters or numbers.

1.3.1   Names of Variables

There are rules for constructing the names of variables.

1.   They can be composed of letters, numbers and full stops.
2.   They must start with a letter.

3.   There is no limit on the length of the name of a variable, but it is not advisable to choose a name longer than twelve characters, if only because the name must be typed every time that the variable is used in the program.

It is a good idea to choose variable names which relate to the contents of the variable. If this is done, it is easier for anyone who reads the program to see what it is intended to do. For example, it would be sensible to use the variable LINE to hold a line of text. It is possible, but not sensible, to hold a line of text in a variable called BLOGGS.

Examples of other variable names:

```
THIS.WORD
CHAR1
WORD.END
```

Note how the full stops are used in variable names which consist of two words. Spaces are not allowed in variable names.

1.3.2   Lower Case Letters in Variable Names

In this book, capital letters are used throughout for variable names. Lower case letters may be used, but it should be noted that the names LINE, Line and Line do not refer to the same variable, but to three different ones.

1.4   Assignment Statements

Assignment statements are the simplest method of putting information into variables. An assignment statement consists of a variable name, followed by an equals sign, followed by whatever is to be assigned. Textual information must be surrounded by matching quotes, either single (') or double ("). Information in quotes is called a *string* or a *literal* and can consist of any characters which are known to the computer.

To assign the string CATS AND DOGS to the variable TEXT

```
TEXT = 'CATS AND DOGS'
```

One variable can also be assigned the contents of another variable.

To assign the contents of the variable CHARS to the variable TEXT

```
TEXT = CHARS
```

After this statement, TEXT and CHARS both have the same contents. The information is not lost from CHARS.

Note the difference between this and

```
TEXT = 'CHARS'
```

where the string CHARS, not the contents of the variable CHARS, is assigned to TEXT.

Whenever an assignment is made, the previous contents of the variable are overwritten, that is they are wiped out by the new information. At the end of the following three statements

```
TEXT = 'CATS AND DOGS'
CHARS = 'MICE'
TEXT = CHARS
```

both TEXT and CHARS contain MICE. CATS AND DOGS has been overwritten.

Note that there must be at least one space on either side of the equals sign. Note also that the statement must not begin in the first character position of the line. It must be preceded by at least one space. The reason for this will be explained later.

1.5   More About Strings

A string may consist of any combination of any of the characters on the computer. The maximum length of a string in SNOBOL varies from one computer to another but is in excess of 10,000 characters.

1.5.1   Lower Case Letters in Strings

Lower case letters can be used in strings.

```
TEXT = 'Cats and dogs'
```

Note that lower case letters are treated as being distinct from their upper case equivalents, although it is possible to write a piece of program which causes them to be treated as equivalent.

1.5.2 . Null String

Initially the contents of a variable are nothing, which is called a *null string* in SNOBOL. A null string is neither zero, nor space, but absolutely nothing at all, i.e. the variable is empty. The following statement assigns the null string to the variable WORD.

```
WORD =
```

The previous contents of WORD, if there were any, are wiped out.

If a variable name is mistyped, a new variable consisting of the mistyped name is created and contains the null string. At the end of the following three statements

```
TEXT = 'CATS AND DOGS'
CHARS = 'MICE'
TEXT = CHRS
```

both TEXT and CHRS contain the null string. CHARS is unchanged and contains MICE.

Mistyped variable names are a common cause of program errors and it is advisable to look for these first when a program does not work.

1.6 Significance of Spaces in the Syntax

To the computer, a space is a character and must be treated like any other character. In general, spaces in a SNOBOL program are part of the syntax and are therefore significant. Care should be taken to insert them in the correct places in the program.

However, the actual number of spaces is not significant in the syntax. An exception is within a string when

```
'CATS AND DOGS'
```

is different from

```
'CATS   AND DOGS'
```

1.7 Order of Execution of Statements

In the examples above the statements are executed in the order in which they are written. Unless instructions are given to the contrary, statements in a program are executed in the order in which they are written. At the end of the following five statements

```
TEXT = 'CATS AND DOGS'
CHARS = 'MICE'
NEWTEXT =
CHARS = TEXT
TEXT = NEWTEXT
```

TEXT and NEWTEXT both contain the null string; CHARS contains CATS AND DOGS.

1.8 Simple Pattern Matching

A simple pattern match statement inspects the contents of one variable to see whether it contains a specific string of characters. Later on we will see how the program can make decisions depending on the success or failure of the match.

To ask if the variable TEXT contains DOGS

```
TEXT 'DOGS'
```

To ask if the variable TEXT contains the letter E

```
TEXT 'E'
```

Matching proceeds in a left to right direction and the first occurrence of the characters sought satisfies the match.

TEXT is technically called the subject of the pattern. The strings DOGS and E are patterns. The pattern may also be another variable.

To ask if the variable TEXT contains the contents of the variable CHARS

```
TEXT CHARS
```

1.9   Match and Replace Statements

The match and replace statement examines the contents of a variable and allows the contents to be changed if they contain a specific string of characters. Only the part that is matched is changed. If the match fails, nothing is changed.

To replace DOGS with MICE in the variable TEXT, if TEXT contains DOGS

```
TEXT 'DOGS' = 'MICE'
```

After the following two statements

```
TEXT = 'CATS AND DOGS'
TEXT 'DOGS' = 'MICE'
```

TEXT contains CATS AND MICE.

Only strings, not words, are identified. After

```
TEXT = 'CATS AND DOGS'
TEXT 'DOG' = 'MICE'
```

TEXT contains CATS AND MICES.

Variable names may be used anywhere in a match and replace statement. For example, the statement

```
TEXT CHARS = NEWTEXT
```

first checks whether the variable TEXT contains the contents of the variable CHARS. If it does, it replaces that part of TEXT which matches the contents of CHARS with the contents of the variable NEWTEXT.

A match and replace statement can be thought of as

pattern   subject   pattern   =   replacement

1.9.1   Deletion Using Match and Replace Statements

Match and replace statements are the most convenient way of deleting information from a string in SNOBOL. The information is replaced by a null string.

To delete the letter I from the variable TEXT, if TEXT contains an I

```
TEXT 'I' =
```

Nothing on the right of the equals sign implies a null string.

If TEXT contains more than one I, only the first I will be deleted. We shall see later how to delete all the I's, if there is more than one.

1.10   The Anchor

The pattern match statements given above assume that SNOBOL is operating in the unanchored mode. This means that the variable is inspected to see whether it *contains* a specific string of characters. When SNOBOL operates in the anchored mode the variable is inspected to see whether it *begins* with a specific string of characters.

The mode of pattern matching can be changed by using a special variable called &ANCHOR. When &ANCHOR is 0, all pattern matching is in the unanchored mode. When &ANCHOR is 1, all pattern matching is in the anchored mode. The value of &ANCHOR holds true for all pattern matches until it is changed, i.e. it behaves like a switch. It is advisable to set an initial value for &ANCHOR at the beginning of every program which uses pattern match statements. If the value is not set at the beginning of a program, an initial value is assumed. This initial value can vary from one computer to another. The value of &ANCHOR may be reset anywhere in a program. In

```
&ANCHOR = 1
TEXT = 'CATS AND DOGS'
CHARS = TEXT
TEXT 'DOGS' = 'MICE'
&ANCHOR = 0
CHARS 'DOGS' = 'MICE'
```

The first match and replace statement

```
TEXT 'DOGS' = 'MICE'
```

fails because TEXT does not begin with DOGS. Consequently TEXT is unchanged. When &ANCHOR is set to 0, the second match and replace statement

```
CHARS 'DOGS' = 'MICE'
```

succeeds and CHARS then contains CATS AND MICE.

1.11   Gotos and Labels

Very rarely does a program need to execute all its statements just once and then finish. It usually needs to repeat some or all of its statements or to execute one set of statements if a pattern succeeds and another if the pattern fails.

1.11.1   Conditional Goto

We have seen in Section 1.9.1 that match and replace statements are used to delete information. In order to delete all the instances of I from the variable TEXT, the match and replace statement must be repeated until the pattern match fails. This is done by a *goto* which is dependent on the success or failure of the pattern match. In

```
      &ANCHOR = 0
AGAIN TEXT 'I' =        :S(AGAIN)
```

the program is told to goto (denoted by a colon) the statement labelled AGAIN, in this case itself, if the pattern match is successful (denoted by S after the colon). When there are no more I's left the pattern match fails and the program goes on to the following statement.

There must be at least one space before the colon. The label of the statement to which the program is to jump or branch is enclosed in round brackets. There are no spaces between the colon and the final bracket. The statement to which the program goes may be anywhere in the program, either before or after the goto, or, as in this example, the actual statement which uses it.

A goto can also be conditional on the failure of a pattern match. In this case F instead of S is used after the colon.

To goto a statement labelled NEW if TEXT does not contain CATS

```
        TEXT 'CATS'       :F(NEW)
```

If TEXT does contain CATS, the pattern succeeds and the next statement executed is the one immediately following. It does not need a label.

Gotos for both success and failure are written as follows

```
        TEXT 'CATS'       :F(NEW)S(OLD)
```

Note that the colon is not repeated and there are no spaces between the colon and the bracket after the second label, in this case OLD. Because the program must jump to either NEW or OLD, the statement following this one can only be accessed if it has a label to which the program can jump from elsewhere.

1.11.2   Statement Labels

A label is an optional tag given to a statement so that other statements may jump to the labelled statement.

1.   Labels are composed of any characters.
2.   Labels must begin with a letter.
3.   Labels must always start in the first character position of a line, and be separated from the rest of the statement by at least one space. Statements which do not have a label begin with at least one space.

END is a special label which must always be the last statement of a SNOBOL program. When it has finished what it is doing the program should go to END in order to terminate correctly.

1.11.3   Unconditional Goto

An unconditional goto is not dependent on the result of a pattern match statement. It is written like a conditional goto without the S or F.

```
        &ANCHOR = 0
        TEXT = 'CATS AND DOGS'
        LETTER = 'E'
MORE    TEXT LETTER          :S(END)
        LETTER = 'A'         :(MORE)
END
```

After the assignment CATS AND DOGS to TEXT and E to LETTER, the pattern match statement

MORE   TEXT LETTER   :S(END)

fails because TEXT does not contain an E. The program continues with the following statement

        LETTER = 'A'

and then jumps back to the statement labelled MORE with the contents of the variable LETTER changed to A. :(MORE) is therefore an unconditional goto. The pattern match then succeeds and the program jumps to the label END.

1.12   Concatenation

The contents of two or more variables may be joined together using a concatenation statement. Strings may also be used in concatenation statements. The variables or strings on the right-hand side of the equals sign are joined together in the order in which they are given and the result is stored in the variable on the left-hand side of the equals sign.

It may be thought of as

      variable   =   *string or variable   string or variable*

where any number of items can be listed on the right-hand side of the equals sign.

        ANIMAL1 = 'CAT'
        ANIMAL2 = 'DOG'
        ANIMAL3 = ANIMAL1 ' ' ANIMAL2

ANIMAL3 now contains CAT DOG. Note the inclusion of a space as an item in the concatenation. Without it ANIMAL3 would contain CATDOG. If the concatenation statement was

        ANIMAL3 = ANIMAL2 ANIMAL1

ANIMAL3 would contain DOGCAT.

1.12.1   Appending Information to Variables

The concatenation statement can also be used to append information to a variable.

        ANIMAL1 = ANIMAL1 'S'

ANIMAL1 now contains CATS.

Remember that the items are concatenated in the order in which they are given.

        ANIMAL2 = 'S' ANIMAL2

ANIMAL2 now contains SDOG.

Any number of variables may be concatenated provided that the maximum length of a string is not exceeded.

1.13 INPUT

So far we have only seen how to process or analyse data which is contained within the program. It is usually more convenient for the program to read data which has already been stored in the computer. In this case, the special variable INPUT is used to transfer or read the data, from where it is stored, into one or more variables. This transfer is always done one line at a time.

To put the contents of the next line of data into the variable LINE

```
LINE = INPUT
```

Note that INPUT is on the right-hand side of the equals sign. The contents of INPUT are being assigned to the variable LINE, rather than vice versa.

Whenever INPUT is used, the next available line of data is accessed. Only one line of data can be accessed at a time by INPUT, no more and no less. If only part of a line is required, that part must be extracted from the input by further SNOBOL statements. (Some ways of doing this are explained in Chapter 2.) If two lines are to be stored in one variable, they must be input separately and then concatenated.

To input two lines of data and store them together in TEXT.

```
LINE1 = INPUT
LINE2 = INPUT
TEXT = LINE1 LINE2
```

This may also be written

```
TEXT = INPUT INPUT
```

When the data is exhausted, a conditional goto detecting input failure is normally used to control what the program has to do next. In a simple case, the program may have finished what it has to do and on reaching the end of the data it should go to END. In more complex programs there will be more processing to do when all the data has been exhausted.

To jump to the statement labelled PROC when INPUT fails

```
LINE = INPUT      :F(PROC)
```

1.13.1 Trimming Input

The input line is padded out to 80 characters with spaces. If these spaces are not required, they can be removed on input by setting the special variable &TRIM to 1 at the beginning of the program. After

```
&TRIM = 1
LINE = INPUT
```

LINE contains everything up to and including the last visible character in the input line. Unless the spaces are specifically required, it is advisable to trim the input to avoid unnecessary pattern searches.

Extra program statements are required to read lines longer than 80 characters.

1.14 OUTPUT

The special variable OUTPUT prints whatever is assigned to it.

To print the contents of the variable LINE

        OUTPUT = LINE

To print the string Results of data analysis

        OUTPUT = 'Results of data analysis'

OUTPUT prints on a new line (the next line) every time that something is assigned to it.

Assigning a null string to OUTPUT causes a blank line to be printed.

E.g.

        OUTPUT =

The following (complete) program prints out each line of its data, one by one.

```
MORE  LINE = INPUT      :F(END)
      OUTPUT = LINE     :(MORE)
END
```

When a line has been dealt with, the program goes to the label MORE to repeat the process on the next and successive lines until input fails.

1.15 &STLIMIT

It is very easy to write a program which has errors which cause it to go into an infinite loop. Some computers have a time limit for each program which, when it is reached, causes the program to stop. In SNOBOL the special variable &STLIMIT can be set to the maximum number of statements which a program is allowed to execute. If this limit is reached, the program stops. It is advisable therefore to begin each program with the statement

        &STLIMIT = 10000

which allows for up to 10,000 statements. This is adequate for most test programs. The number of statements obviously increases in proportion to the number of lines of data which are read and a higher value may be necessary for larger amounts of data. Note that commas are not written in large numbers within the program.

1.16 Layout of a Snobol Program

Labels must always begin in the first character position. Statements which do not have a label must begin with one or more spaces.

Unless extra instructions have been given to the compiler, SNOBOL statements should not extend beyond column 72 on each line. A statement may continue on to second and successive lines by putting a plus sign (+) in the first position of the continuation lines. Statements may be broken over lines only where spaces are used. Strings which continue on to a second line must be closed with quotes and re-opened with quotes on the second line as in

```
      OUTPUT = 'NUMBER OF OCCURRENCES OF THE DEFINITE ARTICLE '
+   'IN THIS POEM'
```

The space at the end of the string on the first line ensures that the string is concatenated correctly. Without it the words ARTICLE and IN would be run together.

Several statements may appear on the same line, in which case they are separated by semicolons. However, beginners are advised to use a separate line for each statement and begin statements about position 6, if they do not have a label. It is much easier to find mistakes if a program is set out neatly.

1.17 Comments

Comment lines are extra lines inserted in a program to describe what the program is doing. They are indicated by an asterisk in the first character position. SNOBOL does not attempt to compile those lines which begin with an asterisk. They are merely printed out exactly as they are input.

A box of comments at the beginning is useful to give an overview of the program. There is no limit on the number of comments which may be inserted in a program. The example program from Section 1.2.2 is repeated here with comments inserted.

```
****************************************************************
*
*   Program to count the number of occurrences of
*   WILLIAM in its data
*
****************************************************************
*
*   Initialisation
*
      &ANCHOR = 0
*
*   Get a line of data
*
MORE  LINE = INPUT                :F(PRINT)
*
*   Look for WILLIAM and count it if found
*
AGAIN LINE 'WILLIAM' =             :F(MORE)
      COUNT = COUNT + 1            :(AGAIN)
*
*   Print result
*
PRINT OUTPUT = 'NUMBER OF OCCURRENCES OF "WILLIAM" IS ' COUNT
END
```

1   Example Programs

1.   This program prints out all the lines which begin with the letter T.

```
******************************************************************
*
*   Program to print out lines which begin with T
*
******************************************************************
*
*   Initialisation
*
      &STLIMIT = 10000
      &ANCHOR = 1
      &TRIM = 1
*
*   Look for line beginning with T and print it
*
MORE  LINE = INPUT        :F(END)
      LINE 'T'            :F(MORE)
      OUTPUT = LINE       :(MORE)
END
```

When a line of data has been input, the statement

```
      LINE 'T'            :F(MORE)
```

asks if the line begins with T (the anchor is turned on). If it does not, the pattern fails and the next instruction is that labelled MORE which causes the next line to be input and the process repeated. If the pattern succeeds the statement

```
      OUTPUT = LINE       :(MORE)
```

is executed before the next line is input.

2.   This program reads two lines of data and prints them out on the same line, repeating the process throughout the data. For the sake of simplicity, it assumes that there is an even number of data lines.

```
******************************************************************
*
*   Program to print out two lines of data on one line
*
******************************************************************
*
      &STLIMIT = 10000
      &TRIM = 1
*
*   Read two lines
*
MORE  LINE1 = INPUT                :F(END)
      LINE2 = INPUT
*
*   Concatenate lines and print them
*
      OUTPUT = LINE1 ' ' LINE2   :(MORE)
END
```

INPUT can only read one line at a time. Every time that something is assigned to OUTPUT, it is printed on a new line, the next line. As the input is trimmed, a space is inserted between LINE1 and LINE2 in the concatenation to avoid the lines being run together.

If there is an odd number of data lines, the program must allow for the special case of one line on its own at the end.

```
***********************************************************************
*
*   Program to print two lines of data on one line
*
***********************************************************************
*
      &STLIMIT = 10000
      &TRIM = 1
*
*   Read two lines
*
MORE   LINE1 = INPUT                    :F(END)
       LINE2 = INPUT                    :F(ONE)
*
*   Concatenate lines and print them
*
       OUTPUT = LINE1 ' ' LINE2   :(MORE)
*
*   Special case - one line at end
*
ONE    OUTPUT = LINE1
END
```

3. This program replaces all occurrences of START in its data with FINISH and prints out all the data under a heading START CHANGED TO FINISH.

```
***********************************************************************
*
*   Program to replace all occurrences of START with FINISH
*
***********************************************************************
*
*   Initialisation and heading
*
      &STLIMIT = 10000
      &TRIM = 1
      &ANCHOR = 0
      OUTPUT = 'START CHANGED TO FINISH'
*
*   Change occurrences of START to FINISH
*
MORE   TEXT = INPUT                     :F(END)
AGAIN  TEXT 'START' = 'FINISH'          :S(AGAIN)
       OUTPUT = TEXT                    :(MORE)
END
```

The unanchored mode is required to find all occurrences of START, not just those at the beginning of a line. Note that it is the characters S T A R T which are replaced, not the word START. If the data contained words such as STARTING, RESTART, STARTLED, they would become FINISHING, REFINISH, FINISHLED.

1   Exercises

At the end of this and most other chapters, there is a small set of exercises to try. All are complete programs and solutions to them are given at the end of this book. The exercises for this chapter all require some text as their data and the solutions assume that they are done on the following poem which we shall call the sonnet.

```
REMEMBER ME WHEN I AM GONE AWAY,
GONE FAR AWAY INTO THE SILENT LAND;
WHEN YOU CAN NO MORE HOLD ME BY THE HAND,
NOR I HALF TURN TO GO YET TURNING STAY.
REMEMBER ME WHEN NO MORE DAY BY DAY
YOU TELL ME OF OUR FUTURE THAT YOU PLANNED:
ONLY REMEMBER ME; YOU UNDERSTAND
IT WILL BE LATE TO COUNSEL THEN OR PRAY.
YET IF YOU SHOULD FORGET ME FOR A WHILE
AND AFTERWARDS REMEMBER, DO NOT GRIEVE:
FOR IF THE DARKNESS AND CORRUPTION LEAVE
A VESTIGE OF THE THOUGHTS THAT ONCE I HAD,
BETTER BY FAR YOU SHOULD FORGET AND SMILE
THAN THAT YOU SHOULD REMEMBER AND BE SAD.
```

1.1   Print out all of the sonnet with a blank line between each line.

1.2   Print out all lines in the sonnet which begin with REMEMBER.

1.3   Print out all of the sonnet changing each occurrence of REMEMBER to FORGET.

1.4   Print out only every alternate line of the sonnet and within these lines delete all the spaces.

2 More About Patterns

2.1 Patterns

The pattern match facility is one of the most powerful and flexible features in SNOBOL. In Chapter 1 we looked at the simplest form of a pattern match statement. Now we shall consider more powerful patterns which can be built up in a number of different ways.

The pattern matching operation can be thought of as moving a cursor or pointer along the subject of the pattern. The cursor is always positioned between two characters.

2.1.1 Uses of Patterns

We have already seen the use of patterns to ask questions (Section 1.8). Patterns can also be used to extract part of the contents of a variable. The section which is extracted can be stored in another variable for further processing.

2.2 LEN

LEN(n) is used in a pattern match statement to match or find something which is n characters long. LEN is what is called a *function* and n is known as the *argument* to LEN and may be a variable or a number.

To match the first five characters in TEXT

        TEXT LEN(5)

The cursor is then positioned after the first five characters.

Using a variable

        TEXT LEN(NUMBER)

In this example, the variable NUMBER must contain a number rather than characters. The contents of NUMBER determine how many characters are matched by LEN. If NUMBER contained 6, six characters would be matched. If it contained 3, three characters would be matched.

2.3 Assignment in a Pattern

The characters which have been found by the pattern may be put into another variable in the following manner

        TEXT LEN(5) . FIVE

This statement puts the first five characters of TEXT into FIVE. The full stop is thus used to make an assignment in a pattern. Note that there must be at least one space on either side of the full stop. The characters are not removed from TEXT.

OUTPUT may be used as the variable to which the assignment is made.

To print out the first ten characters in TEXT

```
TEXT LEN(10) . OUTPUT
```

If the argument to LEN is greater than the number of characters in the pattern subject, the pattern fails and no assignment is made.

2.4 BREAK

BREAK(string) is used in a pattern match statement to match all characters up to, but not including, whichever of the characters in string is encountered first. BREAK is also a function and the string which is its argument may be one or more characters, or a variable containing a string.

To match everything up to the first comma in TEXT

```
TEXT = 'CATS, DOGS, MICE'
TEXT BREAK(',')
```

In

```
TEXT = 'CATS AND DOGS'
TEXT BREAK(',')
```

the pattern fails because BREAK cannot find a comma.

To put everything up to the first comma in TEXT into a variable called SECTION

```
TEXT BREAK(',') . SECTION
```

To match everything up to the first punctuation mark in TEXT

```
TEXT BREAK('.,:;?!')
```

Note that the characters which are to be considered as punctuation marks must be defined. If a space is to be included, the pattern should be written

```
TEXT BREAK('.,:;?! ') . SECTION
```

When the argument to BREAK consists of more than one character, the order of the characters does not matter. BREAK matches up to whichever of them comes first in the pattern subject.

If the first character in the pattern subject is one of those in the argument to BREAK, BREAK succeeds, matching a null string which would be assigned to SECTION.

It is better to use a variable containing a string if the same string is required elsewhere in the program.

```
VOWELS = 'AEIOU'
WORD BREAK(VOWELS) . CONS
```

Here everything up to the first vowel in WORD is put into CONS. It is the fact that VOWELS is the argument to BREAK which makes the order of the characters within it irrelevant. It is important to understand the difference between VOWELS as the argument to BREAK and the following. Depending on the value of &ANCHOR,

```
VOWELS = 'AEIOU'
WORD VOWELS
```

asks if WORD begins with, or contains the string AEIOU, i.e. the letters A E I O U in that order.

```
WORD BREAK(VOWELS)
```

finds everything up to the first vowel in WORD. It does not matter which vowel it is or whether it is followed by more vowels.

BREAK leaves the cursor just before the character which it has found. After

```
TEXT = 'CATS, DOGS, MICE'
TEXT BREAK('ST')
```

the cursor is between the A and T of CATS.

2.4.1   BREAK and the Anchored Mode

SNOBOL works much faster when &ANCHOR is 1. Because it searches from the beginning of the pattern subject up to the first occurrence of one of the characters in its argument, BREAK is another way of looking for one or more specific characters. BREAK can therefore be used in the anchored mode to ask if a variable contains one or more characters.

To ask if TEXT contains a Y, it is better to write

```
&ANCHOR = 1
TEXT BREAK('Y')
```

rather than

```
&ANCHOR = 0
TEXT 'Y'
```

which would produce the same result but take longer.

2.5   SPAN

SPAN(string) is a function which is used in a pattern match statement to match an uninterrupted sequence of any characters which are in its argument regardless of the order in which they occur, or how many times they occur. For this purpose a single character may constitute an uninterrupted sequence. When &ANCHOR is 0, SPAN looks for the first character which is in its argument, then matches everything up to the first character which is not in its argument.

```
&ANCHOR = 0
TEXT SPAN(' ')
```

finds the first sequence of one or more spaces in TEXT.

When &ANCHOR is 1, if the pattern subject begins with a character which is in its argument, SPAN matches everything up to the first character which is not in its argument. If the pattern subject does not begin with a character which is in its argument, SPAN fails.

```
&ANCHOR = 1
TEXT SPAN(' ')
```

matches everything up to the first character in TEXT which is not a space. It fails if TEXT does not begin with a space.

```
&ANCHOR = 0
TEXT SPAN('0123456789')
```

matches the first sequence of digits in TEXT, i.e. the first number.

```
&ANCHOR = 0
TEXT = 'THERE ARE 2021 HITS'
TEXT SPAN('0123456789') . NUM
```

assigns 2021 to NUM. The pattern would fail if &ANCHOR was 1.

Note that if numbers contain decimal points, minus or plus signs, these must be included in the argument to SPAN.

```
&ANCHOR = 0
TEXT = 'AVERAGE: 26.3'
TEXT SPAN('0123456789.') . NUM
```

is needed to find 26.3. If the argument to SPAN did not include a decimal point, it would match only 26.

SPAN leaves the cursor at the end of the string it has matched. After

```
&ANCHOR = 0
TEXT = 'LITTLE CATS'
TEXT SPAN('ST')
```

the cursor is positioned after the second T of LITTLE.

2.6 Complex Patterns

Patterns may consist of more than one pattern element or component.

To find everything between the end of the first five characters of TEXT and the next comma and put it into SECTION

```
TEXT = 'CATS, DOGS, MICE'
TEXT LEN(5) BREAK(',') . SECTION
```

Note that . SECTION refers only to BREAK(','). The characters matched by LEN(5) are not put into SECTION. After these statements SECTION contains DOGS and the preceding space. LEN(5) has matched CATS,.

To find the first digit and the three characters which follow it and put them into AGECODE

```
TEXT BREAK('0123456789') LEN(4) . AGECODE
```

The pattern elements must match strings which are adjacent to each other in the subject of the pattern.

```
TEXT = 'CATS AND DOGS'
TEXT 'S' 'AND'
```

This pattern fails because there is a space, not AND, adjacent to S in the pattern subject.

If it is required to extract two strings which are separated by other characters, an extra pattern element must be inserted to skip over the unwanted characters. This mechanism could be used to extract information from specific columns or character positions within a string. The following statement puts the information in columns 1−3 into FIRST and 9−11 into SECOND. LEN(5) without an assignment is used to skip over columns 4−8.

```
TEXT LEN(3) . FIRST LEN(5) LEN(3) . SECOND
```

SPAN may also be used to skip over unwanted characters if the actual characters are known. In

```
TEXT = 'LONG, SHORT, TALL'
LINE BREAK(',') . FIRST SPAN(' ,') BREAK(',') . SECOND
```

the first BREAK(',') matches LONG and the second BREAK(',') matches SHORT. SPAN(' ,') without an assignment skips over the space and comma between the words LONG and SHORT. The pattern would still match for

```
TEXT = 'LONG,      SHORT, TALL'
```

because SPAN(' ,') skips over all the spaces. In

```
TEXT BREAK(',') . FIRST BREAK(',') . SECOND
```

the second BREAK does not move the cursor as it is already positioned before a comma. The pattern succeeds, assigning the null string to SECOND.

2.6.1   &ANCHOR in Complex Patterns

All the elements in a complex pattern must succeed for the pattern match statement to indicate success. If any one of the elements fails, the pattern may try again if it is permitted to by the value of &ANCHOR. In

```
&ANCHOR = 1
TEXT = 'SENTENCE'
TEXT LEN(2) 'T'
```

the pattern fails because T is not the next character after the first two characters. If &ANCHOR was 0 the pattern would try again beginning at the second character so that LEN(2) matches EN. In this case it would succeed. In

```
&ANCHOR = 0
TEXT = 'SENTENCE'
TEXT LEN(2) . TWO 'C'
```

the pattern makes four unsuccessful attempts to match before LEN(2) is followed by C. This pattern puts the two characters which precede the first C into TWO.

2.7 REM

REM is a special variable. It matches the remainder of a variable after the other pattern elements have been found and is therefore only sensible as the last element in a pattern.

To match everything after the first two characters in TEXT and put it into NEWLINE

```
TEXT LEN(2) REM . NEWLINE
```

To print out everything after the first number in TEXT

```
TEXT SPAN('0123456789') REM . OUTPUT
```

This pattern fails if &ANCHOR is 1 and TEXT does not start with a digit (see Section 2.5).

To match everything after the first comma in TEXT and put it into TEXT

```
TEXT BREAK(',') ',' REM . TEXT
```

Note the use of ',' on its own after BREAK(','). This is to move on one position so that the string which REM matches begins after the comma. LEN(1) is another way of moving the cursor on by one position and should be used when the argument to BREAK consists of more than one character, as in

```
TEXT BREAK('.,:;?!') LEN(1) REM . TEXT
```

2.8 Using BREAK and SPAN to Find Words

SPAN and BREAK may be combined to make complex patterns. In particular a combination of BREAK and SPAN is the best way of extracting words from a string. The anchor should be turned on for this operation.

```
&ANCHOR = 1
LETTERS = 'ABCDEFGHIJKLMNOPQRSTUVWXYZ'
LINE BREAK(LETTERS) SPAN(LETTERS)
```

Here BREAK(LETTERS) matches everything up to the first letter in LINE and SPAN(LETTERS) matches the first group of letters, i.e. the first word.

To put the first word in LINE into a variable called WORD

```
LINE BREAK(LETTERS) SPAN(LETTERS) . WORD
```

When the word starts in the first character position, BREAK(LETTERS) matches the null string. If the program is to inspect each word in turn it must be made to transfer successive words from LINE into WORD. This is done by deleting each word from LINE as it is found and then repeating the statement.

```
LINE BREAK(LETTERS) SPAN(LETTERS) . WORD =
```

This is a match and replace statement (Section 1.9). Everything which has been found by the pattern BREAK(LETTERS) SPAN(LETTERS) . WORD is replaced by the null string. In

```
LINE = 'THE CAT SAT ON THE MAT'
LINE BREAK(LETTERS) SPAN(LETTERS) . WORD
```

the first time that the pattern statement is executed, BREAK(LETTERS) matches a null string and SPAN(LETTERS) matches the word THE which is put into WORD and deleted from LINE. LINE is then

```
' CAT SAT ON THE MAT'
```

beginning with the space before CAT. BREAK(LETTERS) is necessary to move to the C of CAT for the next word. After it has dealt with the first word, here THE, the program would contain a goto taking it back to this statement. The second time that the statement is executed, the word CAT is put into WORD and both CAT and the space before it are deleted from LINE.

BREAK(LETTERS) also deals with any punctuation. If the words are likely to contain accents and other non-alphabetic characters, these characters must be included in LETTERS. The following example allows for upper and lower case letters and the symbols / \ and * to represent accents.

```
UPPERS = 'ABCDEFGHIJKLMNOPQRSTUVXWYZ'
LOWERS = 'abcdefghijklmnopqrstuvxwyz'
ACCENTS = '/\*'
LETTERS = UPPERS LOWERS ACCENTS
LINE BREAK(LETTERS) SPAN(LETTERS) . WORD
```

Note how the three types of letters are concatenated together in LETTERS. They can then also be used separately if required.

In a complex pattern what is on the right of the equals sign replaces in the subject what has been found by the entire pattern. The assignment operator . refers only to the preceding pattern element. If the characters which come between words were to be stored, an assignment would also be necessary for BREAK(LETTERS) as in

```
LINE BREAK(LETTERS) . GAP SPAN(LETTERS) . WORD
```

When all the words in LINE have been dealt with, the statement fails as no more letters can be found. The program would normally then go on to read the next line of data, after dealing with any remaining punctuation in LINE.

Once words have been extracted in this way they may be analysed further individually. The following program prints out all the words which contain a letter Y.

```
*******************************************************************
*
*   Program to print out words which contain Y
*
*******************************************************************
*
*   Initialisation
*
      &STLIMIT = 10000
      &TRIM = 1
      &ANCHOR = 1
      LETTERS = 'ABCDEFGHIJKLMNOPQRSTUVWXYZ'
*
*   Read data and inspect words
*
```

```
MORE   LINE = INPUT       :F(END)
AGAIN  LINE BREAK(LETTERS) SPAN(LETTERS) . WORD =   :F(MORE)
       WORD BREAK('Y')    :F(AGAIN)
       OUTPUT = WORD      :(AGAIN)
END
```

Once a word has been found and is put into the variable WORD, the statement

```
WORD BREAK('Y')
```

asks if the word contains a Y. The words are printed by the statement

```
OUTPUT = WORD
```

one per line. We shall see later how to print them in columns across the page.

2.9 Conditional Value Assignment

We have seen that the operator . is used to transfer whatever a particular pattern element has found into another variable. Every element of a pattern may have a . associated with it but the assignments are only made if the entire pattern matches, that is the assignments are *conditional* on the pattern match. This is in contrast with immediate value assignment (Section 7.3). In

```
TEXT BREAK(',') . NEWTEXT LEN(12) . REST
```

BREAK(',') positions the cursor just before the first comma. If there are less than twelve characters left in TEXT, the pattern fails and no assignment is made to NEWTEXT or to REST. NEWTEXT still contains whatever it contained before the statement was executed.

If there are twelve or more characters after the cursor in TEXT, both assignments are made.

To print out what comes before the first comma and after the second comma in LINE

```
LINE BREAK(',') . OUTPUT ',' BREAK(',') ',' REM . OUTPUT
```

This statement generates two lines of output if the pattern succeeds and none if it fails. Note again the use of ',' to move the cursor past the comma so that the second BREAK(',') moves the cursor up to the second comma.

2.10 Alternation

Patterns may also contain one or more alternatives which must be separated by the alternation symbol (|).

A pattern containing alternatives succeeds as soon as one of the alternatives is found. It fails if none of them is found.

To ask if TEXT contains CAT or DOG

```
TEXT 'CAT' | 'DOG'
```

If TEXT contains DOGS AND CATS the match is satisfied by DOG, the alternative which appears first in the subject of the pattern.

To put the alternative which has been found into ANIMAL

```
TEXT ('CAT' | 'DOG') . ANIMAL
```

The brackets round the alternatives ensure that . ANIMAL refers to both of them. Otherwise it would only refer to DOG and no assignment would be made if CAT was found.

2.11   Assignment of a Pattern to a Variable

A pattern may be defined by assigning the pattern to a variable. That variable can then be used as the pattern in a pattern match statement. This facility saves repeated typing of a complicated pattern. It is also a more efficient way of using SNOBOL, as the form of the pattern which SNOBOL requires for execution is constructed once and stored in the variable. Writing a pattern in the main loop of the program (in-line as it is called) causes the pattern to be constructed each time that it is used.

In

```
ANIMAL = 'CAT' | 'DOG'
TEXT ANIMAL
CHARS ANIMAL
```

both TEXT and CHARS are inspected to see if they contain CAT or DOG.

2.11.1   Building up Pattern Variables

Alternation and concatenation may be used with variables containing patterns.

In this example alternation is used with two pattern variables which themselves contain alternatives.

```
HOUSE.ANIMAL = 'CAT' | 'DOG'
FARM.ANIMAL = 'COW' | 'SHEEP'
ANIMAL = HOUSE.ANIMAL | FARM.ANIMAL
```

The pattern ANIMAL is now CAT or DOG or COW or SHEEP.

Here the pattern variables are concatenated.

```
COLOUR = 'BROWN' | 'BLACK'
PET.ANIMAL = 'CAT' | 'DOG'
ANIMAL1 = COLOUR ' ' PET.ANIMAL
```

ANIMAL1 now matches BROWN CAT, BROWN DOG, BLACK CAT, BLACK DOG.

We could add further pattern definitions to build up patterns.

```
FARM.ANIMAL = 'COW' | 'SHEEP' | 'PIG'
HCOLOUR = 'WHITE' | COLOUR
HORSE = 'HORSE' | 'PONY'
ANIMAL = ANIMAL1 | FARM.ANIMAL | HCOLOUR ' ' HORSE
```

HCOLOUR is now WHITE or BROWN or BLACK and ANIMAL matches any one of the following.

```
BROWN CAT        WHITE HORSE
BROWN DOG        WHITE PONY
BLACK CAT        BROWN HORSE
BLACK DOG        BROWN PONY
COW              BLACK HORSE
SHEEP            BLACK PONY
PIG
```

2.11.2   Pattern Variables with Assignment

A pattern variable may contain assignments.

```
WORDPAT = BREAK(LETTERS) SPAN(LETTERS) . WORD
LINE WORDPAT =
```

If WORDPAT is replaced by its contents, the statement

```
LINE WORDPAT =
```

has exactly the same effect as

```
LINE BREAK(LETTERS) SPAN(LETTERS) . WORD =
```

but is more efficient.

The pattern

```
ANIMAL = (ANIMAL1 | FARM.ANIMAL) . MY.ANIMAL
```

puts into MY.ANIMAL whatever it has matched.

2   Example Programs

1.   This program prints out the first five characters of each line of its data.

```
******************************************************************
*
*    Program to print out the first five characters of each line
*    of data
*
******************************************************************
*
*    Initialisation
*
     &STLIMIT = 10000
     &TRIM = 1
     &ANCHOR = 1
*
*    Read a line and print the first five letters
*
MORE  LINE = INPUT          :F(END)
      LINE LEN(5) . OUTPUT  :(MORE)
END
```

2.   This program prints out all data lines which contain PR or MM or TG in positions 5 and 6.

```
******************************************************************
*
*    Program to print out data lines which contain PR or MM or
*    TG in positions 5 and 6.
*    Code in positions 5 and 6 represents location of paintings
*
******************************************************************
*
*    Initialisation
*
        &STLIMIT = 10000
        &ANCHOR = 1
        &TRIM = 1
        PAT = 'PR' | 'MM' | 'TG'
*
*    Read a line - is it one we want?  If so, print it
*
MORE    LINE = INPUT           :F(END)
        LINE LEN(4) PAT        :F(MORE)
        OUTPUT = LINE          :(MORE)
END
```

The pattern PAT is constructed once at the beginning of the program. LEN(4) is used to skip over the first four characters of LINE. For the pattern to succeed, PAT must begin in column 5 as &ANCHOR is 1. If &ANCHOR is 0 and the pattern failed, it would try again starting at the second character so that LEN(4) skips positions 2, 3, 4, 5 and PAT starts at column 6. If this failed the pattern would try again beginning at position 3 and so on until the end of LINE is reached.

If LEN(4) was also included in the pattern variable PAT, the pattern must be written

```
        PAT = LEN(4) ('PR' | 'MM' | 'TG')
```

to ensure that LEN(4) relates to each of the alternatives. Otherwise the alternatives would be

1.   LEN(4) 'PR'
2.   'MM'
3.   'TG'

i.e. MM and TG would be matched in positions 1 and 2.

The statement

```
        LINE LEN(4) PAT  :F(MORE)
```

would then become

```
        LINE PAT   :F(MORE)
```

Very often data from historical or archaeological research has coded information about specific attributes of an object in different columns or character positions along each line. In this example we could perhaps assume that each line of data represents a painting and positions 5 and 6 of each line record which art gallery the painting is now in, as follows

PR	Prado
MM	Metropolitan Museum
TG	Tate Gallery

The program retrieves all paintings from any one of these galleries.

3.   Suppose that we wanted to retrieve all paintings from these three galleries and any other paintings in any gallery which had been acquired in 1950. If the date of acquisition began in column 8, the program would then be

```
****************************************************************
*
*   Program to print out data lines which contain PR or MM or
*   TG in positions 5 and 6 or 1950 beginning in column 8.
*   Characters in positions 5 and 6 represent location of painting.
*   Date of acquisition begins in column 8
*
****************************************************************
*
*   Initialisation
*
        &STLIMIT = 10000
        &ANCHOR = 1
        &TRIM = 1
        PAT1 = LEN(4) ('PR' | 'MM' | 'TG')
        PAT2 = LEN(7) '1950'
        PAT = PAT1 | PAT2
*
*   Read a line - is it one we want? If so, print it
*
MORE    LINE = INPUT       :F(END)
        LINE PAT           :F(MORE)
        OUTPUT = LINE      :(MORE)
END
```

Note how the two patterns PAT1 and PAT2 are constructed separately and then defined as alternatives in PAT. If a third possibility was also required, it could be defined in a third pattern PAT3 and three alternatives,

        PAT = PAT1 | PAT2 | PAT3

defined for PAT.

In this program, if a line satisfies more than one alternative, it is found for only one of them.

If we wanted only paintings in our three galleries which had been acquired in 1950, one pattern only would be needed.

        PAT = LEN(4) ('PR' | 'MM' | 'TG') LEN(1) '1950'

LEN(1) skips past column 7 so that 1950 begins in column 8.

4. This program prints out all words which begin with A.

```
****************************************************************
*
*   Program to print out all words which begin with A
*
****************************************************************
*
*   Initialisation
*
      &STLIMIT = 10000
      &ANCHOR = 1
      &TRIM = 1
      LETTERS = 'ABCDEFGHIJKLMNOPQRSTUVWXYZ'
      WORDPAT = BREAK(LETTERS) SPAN(LETTERS) . WORD
*
*   Read a line
*
MORE  LINE = INPUT        :F(END)
*
*   Extract words and print those beginning with A
*
AGAIN LINE WORDPAT =      :F(MORE)
      WORD 'A'            :F(AGAIN)
      OUTPUT = WORD       :(AGAIN)
END
```

With a pattern as simple as the string 'A', it is not worth constructing the pattern outside the main loop of the program.

Any program which handles individual words must go through the process of extracting the words from a line one by one.

5. This program prints out all words which contain more than one A. Note the pattern LETPAT which finds more than one A. BREAK('A') must be followed by 'A' to move the cursor past the first A so that it may look for the second. The second BREAK('A') positions the cursor just before the second A and is sufficient to establish that there is more than one A.

```
****************************************************************
*
*   Program to print out all words which contain more than one A
*
****************************************************************
*
*   Initialisation
*
      &STLIMIT = 10000
      &TRIM = 1
      &ANCHOR = 1
      LETTERS = 'ABCDEFGHIJKLMNOPQRSTUVWXYZ'
      WORDPAT = BREAK(LETTERS) SPAN(LETTERS) . WORD
```

```
*
*  Pattern to find more than one A
*
      LETPAT = BREAK('A') 'A' BREAK('A')
*
*  Read a line
*
MORE  LINE = INPUT      :F(END)
*
*  Extract words and print those which contain more than one A
*
AGAIN LINE WORDPAT =    :F(MORE)
      WORD LETPAT       :F(AGAIN)
      OUTPUT = WORD     :(AGAIN)
END
```

2 Exercises

A second set of data is introduced for the exercises in this chapter. From now on some of the exercises will be for the sonnet and some for the new set of data which we shall call the people.

In the people data set, each line represents one person and each person is described by the following characteristics which are called fields: name, father's name, place of birth, date of birth, date of death and occupation. Each person also has a unique identification number. It is wasteful of both time and computer storage to type out the complete names of the places and occupations, if there are only a few possible ones. They can be input in coded form. Dates should also be input in numeric form rather than using the names of the months. The dates here are given in the form: *year, month, day* so that, for example, 12 July 1963 appears as **19630712**.

The information for each person is input as follows

Columns (position in line)

1 – 2	Identification number
3 – 4	Place of birth (see below for abbreviations)
5 – 12	Date of birth
13 – 20	Date of death
21	Occupation (see below for abbreviations)
22 –	Name and father's name. An asterisk separates the name and father's name. Because the names are of varying lengths, it is easier to use a character such as an asterisk to terminate them rather than to fill them up with spaces to the length of the longest name. The surname is given first, followed by a comma, a space and the Christian name. This makes it easier to put the names into alphabetical order.

The data for person number 1, John Smith, son of Fred, a lawyer born in London on 21 June 1890 and died on 3 November 1953 is

```
1LN1890062119531103LSMITH, JOHN*FRED
```

Although this is not easy to read, it is the most economical of both typing effort and computer storage. SNOBOL is one of the best languages for handling data of this kind and it is very easy to use SNOBOL to reproduce it in a more readable form.

The complete set of (hypothetical) people is

```
1LN1890062119531103LSMITH, JOHN*FRED
2NY1900031519680122TBROWN, JAMES*WILLIAM
3SY1898040919520628AJONES, HENRY*PETER
4LN1908120119690115LWILSON, DAVID*JACK
5ED1898031219560902JSCOTT, MICHAEL*HENRY
6NY1888072919621201JJAMES, KEITH*JOHN
7CH1899013119521029DWILLIAMS, PETER*JOHN
8SY1902110419480915LGREEN, GEORGE*FRED
9NY1894091619490227DHARRIS, GEOFFREY*WILLIAM
10TO1903052919600205LROBERTS, DAVID*WILLIAM
11LN1899071319520819DMILES, JOSEPH*JOHN
12TO1902060319690429JWHITE, PETER*GEOFFREY
13NY1906101519630829LEDWARDS, ALAN*HENRY
14CH1898111419591013APETERSON, WILLIAM*GEORGE
```

The abbreviations used are

Places of birth:

```
CH   Chicago
ED   Edinburgh
LN   London
NY   New York
SY   Sydney
TO   Toronto
```

Occupations:

```
A   Accountant
D   Doctor
J   Journalist
L   Lawyer
T   Teacher
```

2.1   Print out all the fields for all the people who were born in London or New York.

2.2   Print out all of the words in the sonnet which contain an L.

2.3   Print out all of the people who were born in London or who were lawyers.

2.4   Print out the people data set in a more readable form, i.e. by putting spaces between the fields. Omit the father's name.

2.5   Write each line of the sonnet backwards, so that the last letter is first and the first letter last.

3 Arithmetic

3.1 Arithmetic Operations

Although SNOBOL is primarily a string-handling language, arithmetic is still needed for some operations. The most obvious of these is counting the number of occurrences of one or more features in the data. Arithmetic is performed by an assignment statement in which the result of the calculation is stored in one variable which appears on the left hand side of the equals sign.

SNOBOL can be used to perform the arithmetic operations of addition, subtraction, multiplication, division and exponentiation. Exponentiation means raising a number to the power of another number.

The following symbols are used for arithmetic operations:

addition	+
subtraction	−
multiplication	*
division	/
exponentiation	**

Spaces are used to separate variables and operators in arithmetic statements as in other forms of assignment statements.

To add 3 to the value of WORD.COUNT and store the result in TOTAL

```
TOTAL = WORD.COUNT + 3
```

Note that the equals sign means 'replace the value of', not equals in the mathematical sense.

3.2 Counting Features in the Data

When running totals are to be kept, for example to record the number of occurrences of a particular feature in the data, a variable is required for each running total. Every time that a new occurrence of each feature is found, the number 1 is added to the relevant variable. When the end of the data is reached, that variable then contains the total number of occurrences found.

A statement such as the following is required to add 1 to the value of COUNT

```
COUNT = COUNT + 1
```

3.3   Integers and Reals

It is important to understand the difference between the two types of numbers. Numbers may be either whole numbers, which are called integers, or numbers containing a decimal point, which are called real numbers or reals. The following are examples of integers

        623 109 5 -62 72

The following are examples of real numbers

        45.69 102.5 0.489 -59.65 72.0

Note that, although they appear to have the same value, 72 and 72.0 are stored differently in the computer because the first is an integer and the second is a real. If both integer and real numbers are used in an arithmetic statement, the result is a real number. An arithmetic statement which operates entirely on integers yields an integer result, even if it is a division. In this case the remainder is lost, i.e. the answer is rounded down to the whole number below rather than rounded up or down to the nearest whole number.

After each of the three following statements

        X = 9 / 3
        X = 10 / 3
        X = 11 / 3

X has the value 3.

Therefore it may be necessary to force one of the numbers to be a real in order to give the correct answer.

        X = 10 / 3.0

yields 3.3333 in X.

This is particularly important in programs which calculate the mean or average number of occurrences of a feature, or which calculate percentages.

Exponentiation is not allowed to the power of a real number, but there are more sophisticated ways of avoiding this problem when calculating, for example, square roots for standard deviations.

3.4   More Arithmetic Statements

More examples of arithmetic statements are given here.

To multiply the contents of V3 by 10 and assign the result to NEWV3

        NEWV3 = V3 * 10

To multiply the contents of V4 by -5 and assign the result to NEWV4

        NEWV4 = V4 * -5

Note that here the minus refers only to 5 and so there is no space between it and 5.

To multiply the contents of X by 0.5 and assign the result to Y

    Y = X * 0.5

Note that the 0 must always be present before the decimal point.

Several arithmetic operators may be included in the same statement. In this case the order of evaluation is exponentiation, multiplication, division, addition, subtraction. If brackets are present, the expressions within the brackets are evaluated first.

Note the difference between

    X = 3 + 2 * 4 + 3

in which the multiplication is evaluated first to give 3 + 8 + 3, that is 14, and

    X = (3 + 2) * (4 + 3)

in which the additions are evaluated first to give 5 * 7, that is 35.

3.4.1   Calculating Percentages

In humanities applications a common arithmetic statement which requires more than one operator is the calculation of a percentage. The following statement assigns to PERC, 27 as a percentage of 86.

    PERC = 100.0 * 27 / 86

Note how integer division is avoided. If all the values were integers, the result would not be exactly accurate. The statement

    PERC = 27 / 86 * 100.0

would produce a wrong result, because the multiplication would be evaluated first. It should be written

    PERC = (27 / 86) * 100.0

3.5   Arithmetic Functions

Comparisons between numeric variables are made using arithmetic functions. These functions, which ask a question, are known as predicate functions.

       GE(X,Y) asks if X is greater than or equal to Y
       GT(X,Y) asks if X is greater than Y
       LT(X,Y) asks if X is less than Y
       LE(X,Y) asks if X is less than or equal to Y
       NE(X,Y) asks if X is not equal to Y
       EQ(X,Y) asks if X is equal to Y

Conditional gotos can be used to control the flow of the program depending on the success or failure of these functions.

To jump to the statement labelled CLEAROUT if COUNT is greater than 20

```
GT(COUNT,20)    :S(CLEAROUT)
```

To go to LAB1 if X and X1 are equal and to go to LAB2 if they are unequal

```
EQ(X,X1)    :S(LAB1)F(LAB2)
```

These functions cause an error if either of the arguments is not numeric.

3.6   Strings and Numbers

Numbers are input as strings and are treated initially as a sequence of characters which happen to be digits. The function SPAN which has a string as its argument is often used to extract numbers from a string. A string which consists entirely of digits, decimal points and plus or minus signs is automatically converted to a number as soon as a numeric operation is performed on it.

In

```
X = '325'
LT(X,400)        :S(YES)
```

the variable X is initially a string containing the characters 3, 2 and 5. It is converted to a number 325 as soon as it is required to perform the numeric function LT on it.

Null strings are converted to 0 when a numeric operation is performed on them. Therefore the initial value of a numeric variable can be assumed to be 0.

3.7   Loops Controlled by Numeric Variables

It is frequently necessary to execute a group of statements a particular number of times. This is one kind of program loop. The loop must be controlled by a variable which counts the number of times that the loop has been executed. An arithmetic function is used to test whether that variable has reached the required total, at which point the loop is terminated.

The following program prints out the first five lines of its data which begin with a T.

```
******************************************************************
*
*   Program to print out the first five lines of data which
*   begin with T
*
******************************************************************
*
*   Initialisation
*
      &STLIMIT = 10000
      &TRIM = 1
      &ANCHOR = 1
```

```
*
*  Read data and print line if it begins with T
*
MORE   LINE = INPUT           :F(END)
       LINE 'T'               :F(MORE)
       OUTPUT = LINE
*
*  Test for five lines
*
       LT(TCOUNT,4)           :F(END)
       TCOUNT = TCOUNT + 1    :(MORE)
END
```

Note how LT is used. The three operations of printing the line, testing the value of TCOUNT and adding 1 to it happen sequentially not simultaneously. The lines are printed before they are counted and so TCOUNT is still 4 when the fifth line has been printed.

The arithmetic function may be combined with an arithmetic statement.

```
       TCOUNT = LT(TCOUNT,4) TCOUNT + 1   :S(MORE)
```

In this case the arithmetic function is executed first. If it succeeds the rest of the statement is executed and the program jumps to the label MORE. If it fails the rest of the statement is not executed, and the program goes on to the following statement.

The program shown above could be rewritten

```
****************************************************************
*
*  Program to print out the first five lines of data which
*  begin with T
*
****************************************************************
*
*  Initialisation
*
       &STLIMIT = 10000
       &TRIM = 1
       &ANCHOR = 1
*
*  Read data and print line if it begins with T
*
MORE   LINE = INPUT           :F(END)
       LINE 'T'               :F(MORE)
       OUTPUT = LINE
*
*  Test for five lines
*
       TCOUNT = LT(TCOUNT,4) TCOUNT + 1   :S(MORE)
END
```

If TCOUNT is set to 1 at the beginning of the program, LT can then test for it to be 5.

```
*******************************************************************
*
*   Program to print out the first five lines of data which
*   begin with T
*
*******************************************************************
*
*   Initialisation
*
      &STLIMIT = 10000
      &TRIM = 1
      &ANCHOR = 1
      TCOUNT = 1
*
*   Read data and print line if it begins with T
*
MORE  LINE = INPUT         :F(END)
      LINE 'T'             :F(MORE)
      OUTPUT = LINE
*
*   Test for five lines
*
      TCOUNT = LT(TCOUNT,5) TCOUNT + 1    :S(MORE)
END
```

Essentially it does not matter which of these ways is used, provided that the
programmer understands the order in which the statements are to be executed and that
the program has dealt with the correct number of items, not one too many or one too
few.

3   Example Programs

1.   This program counts the number of words which begin with a T. Note that with a
program of this kind, the answer must be printed once the end of the data is reached
and so the program does not go to the label END when input fails.

```
*******************************************************************
*
*   Program to count the number of words which begin with T
*
*******************************************************************
*
*   Initialisation
*
      &STLIMIT = 10000
      &ANCHOR = 1
      &TRIM = 1
      LETTERS = 'ABCDEFGHIJKLMNOPQRSTUVWXYZ'
      WORDPAT = BREAK(LETTERS) SPAN(LETTERS) . WORD
```

```
*
*   Read a line
*
MORE  LINE = INPUT            :F(PRINT)
*
*   Extract words and count those which begin with T
*
AGAIN LINE WORDPAT =          :F(MORE)
      WORD 'T'                :F(AGAIN)
      COUNT = COUNT + 1       :(AGAIN)
*
*   Print result
*
PRINT OUTPUT = 'NUMBER OF WORDS BEGINNING WITH A "T" IS '
+     COUNT
END
```

The space at the end of the message NUMBER OF WORDS BEGINNING WITH A "T" IS ensures that the number does not run into the word IS. Otherwise, the message would be printed as

NUMBER OF WORDS BEGINNING WITH A "T" IS106

assuming a value of 106 for COUNT. It is best to print a message of this kind before the total in order to identify it. Without it a statement such as

OUTPUT = COUNT

would print the number on its own and the reader would have no means of knowing what it is. A message is essential for identification if more than one number is to be printed.

2.   To count the words beginning with T in the first ten lines of its data the program would be

```
*******************************************************************
*
*   Program to count the words beginning with T in the first 10
*   lines of data
*
*******************************************************************
*
*   Initialisation
*
      &STLIMIT = 10000
      &TRIM = 1
      &ANCHOR = 1
      LETTERS = 'ABCDEFGHIJKLMNOPQRSTUVWXYZ'
      WORDPAT = BREAK(LETTERS) SPAN(LETTERS) . WORD
*
*   Read a line if we have not yet read 10 lines
*
MORE  LNO = LT(LNO,10) LNO + 1    :F(PRINT)
      LINE = INPUT                :F(ERR)
```

```
*
*   Extract words and count those which begin with T
*
AGAIN LINE WORDPAT =                :F(MORE)
      WORD 'T'                      :F(AGAIN)
      COUNT = COUNT + 1             :(AGAIN)
*
*   Print result
*
PRINT OUTPUT = 'NUMBER OF WORDS BEGINNING WITH A "T" IS '
+      COUNT      :(END)
*
*   Error message if not enough lines
*
ERR   OUTPUT = 'NO RESULT - LESS THAN 10 LINES READ'
END
```

3.   In this example the program calculates the percentage of the words in the first ten lines which begin with T.

```
*****************************************************************
*
*   Program to calculate percentage of words in the first 10 lines
*   which begin with T
*
*****************************************************************
*
*   Initialisation
*
      &STLIMIT = 10000
      &ANCHOR = 1
      &TRIM = 1
      LETTERS = 'ABCDEFGHIJKLMNOPQRSTUVWXYZ'
      WORDPAT = BREAK(LETTERS) SPAN(LETTERS) . WORD
*
*   Read a line if we have not yet read enough
*
MORE  LNO = LT(LNO,10) LNO + 1     :F(CALC)
      LINE = INPUT                 :F(ERR)
*
*   Extract words.  Count those which begin with T and
*   also the total number of words
*
AGAIN LINE WORDPAT =               :F(MORE)
      WORDTOT = WORDTOT + 1
      WORD 'T'                     :F(AGAIN)
      COUNT = COUNT + 1.0          :(AGAIN)
*
*   Calculate percentage and print result
*
CALC  PERC = COUNT * 100 / WORDTOT
      OUTPUT = 'IN THE FIRST 10 LINES ' PERC '% OF '
+   'WORDS BEGIN WITH "T"'          :(END)
```

```
*
*   Error message if not enough lines read
*
ERR    OUTPUT = 'NO RESULT - LESS THAN 10 LINES READ'
END
```

Note that COUNT is a real number to avoid integer division. When the program has processed enough data it does the calculation before printing the result. Note how the parts of the message are concatenated in the OUTPUT statement. If PERC was 7.3, the message would be

```
IN THE FIRST 10 LINES 7.3% OF WORDS BEGIN WITH "T"
```

3 Exercises

3.1 Count the number of words in the sonnet.
3.2 What percentage of the people are lawyers?
3.3 Count the number of people who were more than 60 years old when they died.
3.4 Print out all the words in the first ten lines of the sonnet which contain an R.

4 More Functions

SNOBOL contains many other functions. Some of these functions are pattern structures like SPAN and BREAK. Others are predicate functions which ask a question. A third category performs some computation and returns a value which must be assigned to another variable.

4.1 Pattern Functions

Pattern functions can only be used within patterns. Although the function is itself a pattern, the argument is either a string or an integer. The argument must not be another pattern such as an alternative.

4.1.1 ANY

ANY(string) matches any character appearing in its argument. Effectively it defines single character alternatives. When these are required, it is more efficient to use ANY than a pattern containing alternation. In other words ANY('AB') and 'A' | 'B' would produce the same result, but ANY('AB') is preferable.

To find the first vowel in TEXT and put it into VOWEL

```
&ANCHOR = 0
TEXT ANY('AEIOU') . VOWEL
```

To ask if TEXT begins with a vowel

```
&ANCHOR = 1
TEXT ANY('AEIOU')
```

4.1.2 NOTANY

NOTANY(string) is a pattern function which matches any single character not in the string given.

To find the first character which is not a vowel in TEXT and put it into NONVOWEL

```
&ANCHOR = 0
LINE NOTANY('AEIOU') . NONVOWEL
```

This finds not just consonants, but any other character on the computer, including lower case a e i o u.

To ask if TEXT does not begin with a vowel

```
&ANCHOR = 1
TEXT NOTANY('AEIOU')
```

4.1.3 TAB

TAB(integer) matches as many characters as are needed to move the cursor from its current position to the point in the subject string indicated by its argument.

        LINE TAB(5) . CHARS

moves the cursor to position 5, that is between characters 5 and 6 and assigns to CHARS the characters from the beginning of LINE up to position 5. It will be seen that this has exactly the same effect as

        LINE LEN(5) . CHARS

However TAB differs from LEN in that the number which is its argument is a character position measured from the beginning of the pattern subject. TAB(5) matches up to character position 5. LEN(5) matches the next five characters. The difference is apparent when TAB and LEN are not the first elements in a pattern. In

        LINE = 'THE CAT SAT ON THE MAT'
        LINE BREAK('C') TAB(7) . CHARS1
        LINE BREAK('C') LEN(7) . CHARS2

TAB(7) matches from the cursor position reached by BREAK('C') up to position 7 and therefore assigns CAT to CHARS1. LEN(7) matches the next seven characters after the position reached by BREAK('C') and therefore assigns CAT SAT to CHARS2.

4.1.4 RTAB

RTAB(integer) is similar to TAB, but its argument counts from the right of the subject string instead of the left. RTAB therefore matches from the current cursor position up to the point where integer characters are left in the subject string.

        LINE RTAB(3) . TEXT

puts into TEXT all but the last three characters of LINE.

        LINE BREAK('Y') RTAB(1) . TEXT

puts into TEXT everything from the first Y up to but not including the last character in LINE.

RTAB can therefore be used to inspect the ends of strings.

        LINE RTAB(1) 'Y'

asks if LINE ends with a Y. RTAB(1) matches everything up to the last character, for which a Y is required for the pattern to succeed.

        LINE RTAB(3) 'P'

asks if a P is the third character from the end.

&ANCHOR can be set to 1 for these patterns.

4.1.5   POS

POS(integer) is used to test whether the cursor is at the character position defined by its argument. It does not itself match anything and therefore cannot be used with a conditional value assignment.

        LINE SPAN(' ') POS(6)

succeeds if there is a span of blanks up to position 6, i.e. LINE begins with six blanks. When &ANCHOR is 0, it succeeds if there is a run of blanks up to position 6 but not necessarily from the beginning of the string. POS(0) has the same effect as setting &ANCHOR to 1 and can be used to anchor one pattern if the rest of the program is in the unanchored mode.

        LINE POS(0) 'A'

asks if LINE begins with A.

4.1.6   RPOS

RPOS(integer) tests whether the cursor is at the character position defined by its argument counting from the right. RPOS(0) is zero character positions from the right-hand end of the string, i.e. immediately after the last character.

Patterns using RPOS must have &ANCHOR set to 0. If &ANCHOR is set to 1, the match is made against the beginning of the string as well.

        &ANCHOR = 1
        LINE 'Y' RPOS(0)

asks if LINE begins and ends with Y, i.e. if it consists of only the single character Y.

        &ANCHOR = 1
        DATE = '1066'
        DATE SPAN('0123456789') RPOS(0)

asks if DATE consists only of digits. A pattern such as this can be useful in a program which verifies data.

        &ANCHOR = 1
        DATE = '10A6'
        DATE SPAN('0123456789')

would not be sufficient because the span of digits would terminate at the A, but the pattern would still succeed. In

        &ANCHOR = 1
        LINE BREAK('Y') RPOS(1)

the pattern succeeds if the only Y in LINE is its last character. RTAB could not be used here because in

        LINE RTAB(1) 'Y'

there may be other instances of Y in the characters matched by RTAB.

4.1.7   Difference Between LEN, POS and TAB

Beginners often confuse LEN, POS and TAB. It is useful to remember that LEN(n) finds the next n characters. TAB(n) finds all the characters from the current cursor position up to position n. POS(n) asks if the cursor is at position n. Both LEN and TAB can have conditional value assignments. POS cannot be followed by a conditional value assignment as it does not itself match anything.

RTAB(n) finds all the characters from the current cursor position to position n counting from the end of the pattern subject. RPOS(n) asks if the cursor is at position n counting from the end of the pattern subject. RTAB can have a conditional value assignment but RPOS cannot.

4.2   Predicate Functions

Predicate functions ask a question by comparing two arguments. A statement which includes a predicate function usually has a conditional goto depending on the success or failure of the predicate function.

A predicate function can also be used in combination with another statement. (See Section 3.7 for the use of numeric predicates in this way.) The rest of the statement is only executed if the predicate function succeeds.

4.2.1   DIFFER

DIFFER has two arguments which may be of any type. It fails if its two arguments are identical. It is mostly used to compare strings.

To jump to the label NEXT if WORD and 'AND' are different

```
DIFFER(WORD,'AND')  :S(NEXT)
```

To print WORD and go to the label NEXT if WORD and 'AND' are different

```
OUTPUT = DIFFER(WORD,'AND') WORD      :S(NEXT)
```

Note that the number 123 and the string '123' are considered to be different by DIFFER, but not by the numeric predicate function NE (Section 3.5) which, like all the numeric predicate functions, first converts its arguments to numbers. As numbers are always input as strings, it is advisable to use the numeric functions for testing numbers.

4.2.2   IDENT

IDENT has two arguments which may be of any type. It succeeds if its two arguments are identical.

To jump to the label NEXT if WORD and 'AND' are identical

```
IDENT(WORD,'AND')   :S(NEXT)
```

This is the best way of looking for a particular word.

    WORD 'AND'

asks if WORD begins with AND and would also match words such as ANDANTE, ANDREW etc.

If the second argument is missing, it is assumed to be a null string.

    IDENT(WORD)

asks if WORD is null.

The following statement assigns NEXTWORD to WORD if WORD is null.

    WORD = IDENT(WORD) NEXTWORD

The string '123' and the number 123 are treated as being different by IDENT. EQ (Section 3.5) converts '123' to a number and treats them as being the same. EQ should therefore be used for comparing numbers and IDENT for comparing strings.

4.2.3   LGT

LGT(string1,string2) tests whether string1 is lexically greater than string2, that is if string1 comes after string2 in alphabetical order.

SNOBOL has an in-built alphabetical order, called the collating sequence, which is adequate only for simple data. The collating sequence includes all non-alphabetic characters such as punctuation and mathematical characters. Upper case letters are treated as being different from their lower case equivalents. Spaces are significant. The collating sequence varies from one computer to another and is stored in a special variable called &ALPHABET whose contents may be printed with a statement such as

    OUTPUT = &ALPHABET

in most versions of SNOBOL. The value of &ALPHABET may be altered in some versions of SNOBOL . If this is possible, it is a very convenient way of handling non-standard alphabets such as transliterated Greek.

To jump to LAB1 if the contents of WORD1 come after the contents of WORD2

    LGT(WORD1,WORD2)   :S(LAB)

The strings may be of any length and therefore may consist of several or many words. In

    TEXT1 = 'THE CAT SAT ON THE MAT'
    TEXT2 = 'THE CAT SAT ON THE RUG'
    LGT(TEXT1,TEXT2)   :S(YES)

LGT fails, indicating that TEXT1 is not lexically greater than TEXT2. This happens only after the strings have been compared as far as MAT and RUG. If there was an extra space in one of the strings, as in

    TEXT1 = 'THE CAT SAT ON THE MAT'

the result of the comparison might be different depending on the collating sequence of the computer, as the extra space would be treated as a character in the comparison and would be compared with the C of CAT.

The following statement prints L̲INE if WORD1 comes after WORD2 in alphabetical order.

```
OUTPUT = LGT(WORD1,WORD2) LINE
```

4.3 Functions Which Return a Value

Functions which return a value perform some process on their arguments the result of which is a number or a string. The number or string is usually assigned to another variable.

4.3.1 DUPL

DUPL(string,integer) duplicates the first argument the number of times specified by the second argument. It is particularly useful for formatting lines of output.

To print ten asterisks

```
OUTPUT = DUPL('*',10)
```

To print the contents of WORD after ten spaces

```
OUTPUT = DUPL(' ',10) WORD
```

This is the normal way of producing a margin on the left of the page.

To print the string /* ten times

```
OUTPUT = DUPL('/*',10)
```

Note that this generates twenty characters because the string which is to be duplicated itself consists of two characters.

```
OUTPUT = DUPL('/*',X)
```

duplicates /* X times.

The second argument to DUPL may be an arithmetic expression which yields an integer.

To assign X − 1 spaces to TEXT

```
TEXT = DUPL(' ',X − 1)
```

4.3.2 REMDR

REMDR(integer1,integer2) returns the remainder after dividing integer1 by integer2. After

```
X = 5
Y = 3
Z = REMDR(X,Y)
```

Z has the value 2.

4.3.3   REPLACE

REPLACE(string1,string2,string3) replaces all occurrences of string2 within string1 with the corresponding character in string3.

To replace all occurrences of A with E in LINE and assign the result to LINE2

```
LINE = 'ABAC'
LINE2 = REPLACE(LINE,'A','E')
```

LINE2 now contains EBEC.

String2 and string3 may contain more than one character. In this case each of the characters in string2 must have a character corresponding to it in string3.

To replace all occurrences of A with E and all occurrences of I with O in LINE and assign the result to LINE2

```
LINE = 'ABACIGIH'
LINE2 = REPLACE(LINE,'AI','EO')
```

LINE2 now contains EBECOGOH.

An instruction such as

```
LINE2 = REPLACE(LINE,'AE','EA')
```

transposes occurrences of A and E correctly. If this is written as two statements

```
LINE2 = REPLACE(LINE,'A','E')
LINE2 = REPLACE(LINE2,'E','A')
```

all occurrences of both A and E become A, as there is no means of knowing which were the original occurrences of A.

The following statements replace all upper case letters with their lower case equivalents in TEXT

```
UPPERS = 'ABCDEFGHIJKLMNOPQRSTUVWXYZ'
LOWERS = 'abcdefghijklmnopqrstuvwxyz'
TEXT = REPLACE(TEXT,UPPERS,LOWERS)
```

For single character replacements it is much better to use REPLACE than a match and replace statement.

4.3.4   SIZE

SIZE(string) returns an integer count of the number of characters in its string argument.

To assign the size of LINE to LINELEN

```
LINELEN = SIZE(LINE)
```

SIZE can be used in an arithmetic expression.

To add the size of WORD to WORDTOT

```
WORDTOT = WORDTOT + SIZE(WORD)
```

A function which returns a value may be used as the argument to another function. In the following statement the number of times which * is duplicated is determined by the size of TEXT.

```
OUTPUT = DUPL('*',SIZE(TEXT))
```

4.3.5   TRIM

TRIM(string) removes spaces from the end of its argument. These spaces are sometimes called *trailing* spaces.

To remove spaces at the end of LINE

```
LINE = TRIM(LINE)
```

4   Example Programs

1.   This program prints out words which end in LY or LEY or which have P as the third letter from the end.

```
*******************************************************************
*
*   Program to print out words which end in LY or LEY or
*   which have P as the third letter from the end
*
*******************************************************************
*
*   Initialisation
*
      &STLIMIT = 10000
      &ANCHOR = 1
      &TRIM = 1
      LETTERS = 'ABCDEFGHIJKLMNOPQRSTUVWXYZ'
      WORDPAT = BREAK(LETTERS) SPAN(LETTERS) . WORD
*
*   Patterns to find the words we want
*
      LYWORDS = RTAB(2) 'LY' | RTAB(3) 'LEY'
      PWORDS = RTAB(3) 'P'
      PAT = LYWORDS | PWORDS
*
*   Read a line and look for words
*
MORE  LINE = INPUT            :F(END)
AGAIN LINE WORDPAT =          :F(MORE)
      WORD PAT                :F(AGAIN)
      OUTPUT = WORD           :(AGAIN)
END
```

The two patterns are defined as alternatives in PAT. RTAB is used to move the cursor to the appropriate place in the pattern subject. It must be repeated in LYWORDS because LY needs RTAB(2) and LEY needs RTAB(3).

2.   This program finds the average length of words in its data.

```
******************************************************************
*
*   Program to calculate the average length of words
*
******************************************************************
*
*   Initialisation
*
      &STLIMIT = 10000
      &ANCHOR = 1
      &TRIM = 1
      LETTERS = 'ABCDEFGHIJKLMNOPQRSTUVWXYZ'
      WORDPAT = BREAK(LETTERS) SPAN(LETTERS) . WORD
*
*   Read a line and look for words
*
MORE  LINE = INPUT          :F(PRINT)
AGAIN LINE WORDPAT =        :F(MORE)
*
*   Count total number of words in WDTOT
*   and number of letters in WDLENGTH
*
      WDTOT = WDTOT + 1.0
      WDLENGTH = WDLENGTH + SIZE(WORD)    :(AGAIN)
*
*   Calculate average and print result
*
PRINT WDAV = WDLENGTH / WDTOT
      OUTPUT = DUPL(' ',10) 'AVERAGE LENGTH OF WORDS IS ' WDAV
END
```

Note that WDTOT is a real number in order to avoid integer division. When the program has reached the end of the data, it does the calculation before printing the result. The message is preceded by ten spaces to indent it from the edge of the page.

It would be permissible to combine the last two statements as follows.

```
PRINT OUTPUT = DUPL(' ',10) 'AVERAGE LENGTH OF WORDS IS '
+        WDLENGTH / WDTOT
```

3.   This program converts data which is in upper case only to upper and lower case. In the upper case version of the data, a dollar sign ($) precedes all letters which are genuinely upper case and must be kept as such.

```
******************************************************************
*
*   Program to convert text in upper case only to
*   upper and lower case.
*   True capitals are preceded by $
*
******************************************************************
*
*   Initialisation
*
      &STLIMIT = 10000
      &ANCHOR = 1
      &TRIM = 1
      UPPERS = 'ABCDEFGHIJKLMNOPQRSTUVWXYZ'
      LOWERS = 'abcdefghijklmnopqrstuvwxyz'
*
*   Read a line
*
MORE  LINE = INPUT          :F(END)
*
*   Break up line around capital marker ($)
*
AGAIN LINE BREAK('$') . FIRST '$' LEN(1) . CAP
+     REM . REST            :F(LAST)
*
*   Convert FIRST to lower case
*
      NEWLINE = NEWLINE REPLACE(FIRST,UPPERS,LOWERS) CAP
*
*   Deal with next bit of line
*
      LINE = REST            :(AGAIN)
*
*   End of capitals in LINE. Convert last section
*   and print NEWLINE
*
LAST  NEWLINE = NEWLINE REPLACE(LINE,UPPERS,LOWERS)
      OUTPUT = NEWLINE
*
*   Empty NEWLINE before doing next line
*
      NEWLINE =               :(MORE)

END
```

Within each line, BREAK('$') is used to find all the text up to $. This text is put into FIRST and then the REPLACE function is used to convert it to lower case. The character following $ is stored in CAP and left unchanged. A new version of the line is built up in NEWLINE. Each new section of the line is concatenated into NEWLINE when it has been converted. At the end of all the capital markers in a line the program goes to the label

LAST where it converts the last remaining section of the line before printing NEWLINE. Because information is being concatenated into it, NEWLINE is set to the null string before the next line is dealt with.

4   Exercises

4.1   Count the number of occurrences of the word YOU in the sonnet and print the result indented by 10 spaces.

4.2   Find all the words in the sonnet which end in S or Y.

4.3   Print out the names and identification numbers of the people with the names converted to lower case except for the initial letters. The names should be in the form: *Christian name, surname.*

4.4   Find the word which comes first in alphabetical order in each line of the sonnet.

5 Arrays and Tables

5.1 Multiple Data Objects

So far in our programs we have used simple variables, each of which is a single object containing either a string, an integer, a real number or a pattern. It is often useful to have a number of objects collected together under the same name, for example if we wanted to store information about every word in a text. SNOBOL provides ways of storing data in this way.

5.2 Arrays

A series of objects which can be referenced in numerical order by the same name is called an array. Each object within the array is called an array element and it has an index number called a subscript which uniquely identifies it. The simplest form of array can be thought of as a row of objects, notionally contiguous.

This diagram

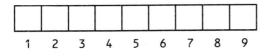

shows an array of nine elements with their subscripts.

The array could be used, for example, for recording how many words have one letter, how many have two and so on up to nine. Element number 1 would record the number of one-letter words, element number 2 two-letter words and so on.

An array must first be created by the function ARRAY which normally has only one argument, the size of the array.

To create an array A with twenty elements

```
A = ARRAY(20)
```

An array must have been created before any attempt is made to use any of its elements. It is sensible to put a statement which creates an array with all the other definitions at the beginning of a program.

5.2.1 Array Subscripts

The numerical subscript of an array element is enclosed in < > after the array name. The array element can be used anywhere where a simple variable is permitted.

To assign the contents of WORD to element number 5 of A

```
A<5> = WORD
```

A variable containing an integer number or arithmetic expression which yields an integer number may also be used as an array subscript.

To assign the contents of WORD to the Ith element of A

```
A<I> = WORD
```

Therefore if I is 2, WORD is put in the second element of A. If I is 4, the fourth element of A is used and so on.

An arithmetic expression which yields an integer may also be used.

To assign the contents of WORD to the element of A indicated by the expression I + 2

```
A<I + 2> = WORD
```

If I is 2, the fourth element of A is used. If I is 0, the second element is used and so on.

Successive elements of an array can therefore be accessed by adding 1 to the value of the subscript. The following section of program puts words into the array A, one per element until 100 words have been stored. If there are less than 100 words all the words are stored.

```
******************************************************************
*
*   Program to store words in successive elements of an array
*
******************************************************************
*
* Initialisation
*
      &ANCHOR = 1
      &STLIMIT = 10000
      &TRIM = 1
      A = ARRAY(100)
      I = 1
      LETTERS = 'ABCDEFGHIJKLMNOPQRSTUVWXYZ'
      WORDPAT = BREAK(LETTERS) SPAN(LETTERS) . WORD
*
* Read a line
*
MORE  LINE = INPUT             :F(PROC)
*
* Get a word and load it into A
*
AGAIN LINE WORDPAT =           :F(MORE)
      A<I> = WORD
*
* Test for reaching 100 words
*
      I = LT(I,100) I + 1      :S(AGAIN)
PROC
```

Note that an initial value for the subscript must be set. It is *not* assumed to be 1.

If the value of the subscript is outside the range of the array, a statement failure occurs which can be detected to control the flow of the program. In the following section of program, an array COUNTS is used in such a way that COUNTS<1> records the number of words which have one letter, COUNTS<2> records words which have two letters etc., up to ten letters. If a word is longer than ten letters, a statement failure occurs and a message is printed.

```
************************************************************
*
*   Program to count number of words of one letter, two letters,
*   three letters, and so on
*
************************************************************
*
*   Initialisation
*
        &ANCHOR = 1
        &TRIM = 1
        &STLIMIT = 10000
        COUNTS = ARRAY(10)
        LETTERS = 'ABCDEFGHIJKLMNOPQRSTUVWXYZ'
        WORDPAT = BREAK(LETTERS) SPAN(LETTERS) . WORD
*
*   Read a line of data
*
MORE    LINE = INPUT                :F(PROC)
*
*   Get a word and calculate its size
*
AGAIN   LINE WORDPAT =              :F(MORE)
        N = SIZE(WORD)
*
* Add 1 to the element of COUNT for that size
*
        COUNTS<N> = COUNTS<N> + 1            :S(AGAIN)
*
* Error if word is too long
*
        OUTPUT = '*******ERROR - WORD ' WORD ' IS TOO LONG'
+           :(AGAIN)
PROC
```

SIZE(WORD) is stored in N to avoid computing it twice, which would be the case if the statement

```
        COUNTS<SIZE(WORD)> = COUNTS<SIZE(WORD)> + 1    :S(AGAIN)
```

was written instead of

```
        N = SIZE(WORD)
        COUNTS<N> = COUNTS<N> + 1            :S(AGAIN)
```

Note that it is not necessary for each element of an array to contain the same type of data. It is permissible for some elements to contain strings, some to contain patterns, and some to contain numbers. This is unlikely, however, to be a very sensible way of organising a program.

5.2.2   Initialising Arrays

The initial value of each element of an array may be preset by using a second argument to the ARRAY function.

To create an array A of 10 elements each containing a *

        A = ARRAY(10,'*')

To create an array B of 20 elements each containing the number 1

        B = ARRAY(20,1)

If the second argument is omitted, the initial value is a null string.

5.2.3   Multi-Dimensional Arrays

An array may have more than one dimension.

To create an array B of 5 rows by 3 columns

        B = ARRAY('5,3')

Such an array, which has two dimensions, can be visualised as follows.

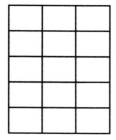

Note the use of apostrophes in the statement which creates the array. Without them the statement would create an array B of five elements, each set to the initial value 3.

When an array has more than one dimension there must be a subscript for each dimension.

To assign the contents of WORD to row 3, column 2 of C

        C<3,2> = WORD

Thus

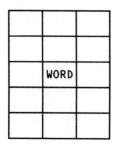

The subscripts should always correspond to the same dimension.

    C<2,3> = WORD

would put WORD in row 2 column 3 of C.

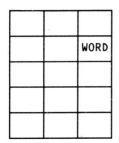

To assign the contents of LINE to row I column J of TEXT

    TEXT<I,J> = LINE

The statement fails if either I or J is out of range. Some more program statements would be necessary to find out which of the two was outside the range.

5.2.4   Unusual Arrays

The arrays we have seen so far all have 1 as the lowest numbered subscript, the *lower bound* of the array. It is possible to have an array whose subscripts do not begin at 1. In this case the lower and upper bounds of the subscript range must be given when the array is created.

    A = ARRAY('-3:4')

creates an array A with lower bound -3 and upper bound 4. 0 is a value for a subscript and so this array has eight elements.

    B = ARRAY('-2:6,101:200')

creates a two-dimensional array B in which the first dimension is numbered from -2 to 6 and the second is numbered from 101 to 200.

An unusual array can be initialised as follows

    B = ARRAY('-2:6,101:200','1')

where all elements are set to 1.

Arrays beginning at 1 are by far the most usual but it is useful to be aware of these more unusual forms particularly when counts or other information are to be stored for particular numbers, as in the program given above which uses SIZE(WORD) to calculate the subscript, but where the numbers are all expected to be much greater than 1.

5.2.5   Size of Arrays

There is no limit on the number of dimensions in an array or on the size of each dimension, other than the overall space limitations within the computer. However,

SNOBOL has other ways of storing multiple data objects. In many circumstances, particularly when a substantial part of the array is likely to be empty, another data structure is more suitable, either a table (Section 5.3) or a user-defined datatype (Chapter 8).

5.2.6   Printing Arrays

When an array is to be printed, each element must be printed separately by assigning it to OUTPUT. The entire contents of an array A cannot be printed by a statement such as

```
        OUTPUT = A
```

The following section of program prints the contents of array A, one element per line. A is a one-dimensional array with lower bound 1.

```
        I = 1
NEXT    OUTPUT = A<I>        :F(END)
        I = I + 1            :(NEXT)
END
```

The value of I is initially set to 1 so that

```
        OUTPUT = A<I>
```

prints A<1> the first time that it is executed. The value of I is incremented by 1 and the program loops back to NEXT to print A<2> and so on until I is out of range within the size of the array. At that point

```
        OUTPUT = A<I>
```

fails and the program goes to END. Two subscripts are needed for a two-dimensional array. The following statements print an array B of 3 by 5 elements

```
        I = 1
INCRJ   J = 1
NEXT    OUTPUT = B<I,J>        :F(END)
        J = LT(J,5) J + 1      :S(NEXT)
        I = I + 1              :(INCRJ)
END
```

Note how LT is used to test the value of J. The LT statement is needed to ensure that only one of the subscripts, here I, is detected out of range in the OUTPUT statement.

5.3   Tables

A table is another way of collecting together a number of objects under the same name. It differs from an array in three respects:

1.   It can have only one dimension.
2.   The number of its elements is not fixed when it is created.
3.   The value of any kind of variable, not just an integer, can be used as a table subscript.

A table is created by the function TABLE which usually has no arguments.

To create a table T

```
T = TABLE()
```

Note that the brackets must be included, even if they are empty. This creates a table which initially has no elements. SNOBOL expands the table whenever a new element is required for it.

If the approximate size of a table is known, it is more efficient to create it to be that size.

To create a table LETTERS consisting of 26 elements

```
LETTERS = TABLE(26)
```

A table which has been created to be a certain size can still be expanded if necessary.

5.3.1 Table Subscripts

The subscript or reference of a table element may be any data type, but it is most usually a string or a variable containing a string.

To assign the number 1 to the element of T referenced by the letter A

```
T<'A'> = 1
```

To add 1 to the element of T referenced by the letter A

```
T<'A'> = T<'A'> + 1
```

More usually the table subscript is itself a variable. Each time that the contents of that variable change, a different table element is accessed.

To add 1 to the element of T referenced by the contents of the variable LETTER

```
T<LETTER> = T<LETTER> + 1
```

If LETTER contained A, the element T<'A'> would be incremented. If LETTER contained B, T<'B'> would be incremented and so on. It is important to understand the difference between T<'A'> where the letter A is the table subscript and T<A> where the contents of A are the subscript.

Table subscripts may also be numbers. In this case the number 123 and the string '123' are treated as different when referencing a table. Care must therefore be taken if some table subscripts are computed and others are extracted from the data as strings. It is better to use a table than an array if the numbers cover a wide range in value and there are many values for which nothing is stored.

5.3.2 Storing Data in Tables

A table is most useful when an initial pass is made through the data to collect up information from it. In the simplest case it could be used to count the number of occurrences of each character using a separate table element to keep the running total for each character. We can see how information is put into the table in the following section of program

```
****************************************************************
*
*   Program to store character counts in a table
*
****************************************************************
*
*   Initialisation
*
        &ANCHOR = 1
        &TRIM = 1
        &STLIMIT = 10000
        T = TABLE()
        LINE = 'THE CAT SAT ON THE MAT'
*
*   Count characters
*
AGAIN LINE LEN(1) . CH =          :F(PRINT)
        T<CH> = T<CH> + 1         :(AGAIN)
PRINT
```

The characters are picked off LINE one by one and stored in CH. When a new value of CH is encountered, a new table element is created and 1 added to it. When CH has a value which it has had before, the program recognises that a table element already exists for that character and merely adds 1 to it. When the program reaches the label PRINT, each element of the table T is subscripted by a character and contains the count for that character.

The table can be thought of as being built up as follows

After one character

After five characters

1	1	1	1	1
'T'	'H'	'E'	' '	'C'

Remember that space is treated just like any other character. After ten characters, some characters have been repeated and the table would be

2	1	1	2	1	2	1
'T'	'H'	'E'	' '	'C'	'A'	'S'

When the end of LINE is reached the table is

5	2	2	5	1	3	1	1	1	1
'T'	'H'	'E'	' '	'C'	'A'	'S'	'O'	'N'	'M'

It has one element for each different character and within that element, a number indicating how many times that character occurs. The diagrams show how a table is expanded as more information is loaded into it but they are not an entirely true representation of what happens. When SNOBOL constructs a table it uses a technique called hashing to generate the subscripts which it needs to reference the table. This is very efficient in computer terms, but it means that within the table the elements are not in the order in which they have been created, but are stored in an apparently random order.

A similar process can be used to store the number of occurrences of each different word in the data.

```
**********************************************************************
*
*  Program to store word counts in a table
*
**********************************************************************
*
*  Initialisation
*
       &ANCHOR = 1
       &TRIM = 1
       &STLIMIT = 10000
       LETTERS = 'ABCDEFGHIJKLMNOPQRSTUVWXYZ'
       WORDPAT = BREAK(LETTERS) SPAN(LETTERS) . WORD
       T = TABLE()
       LINE = 'THE CAT SAT ON THE MAT AND THE DOG SAT ON THE RUG'
*
*  Count words
*
AGAIN LINE WORDPAT =             :F(PRINT)
       T<WORD> = T<WORD> + 1  :(AGAIN)
PRINT
```

When this program reaches the label PRINT, each element of the table T is subscripted by a word and contains the count for that word. At the end of the program, the table can be visualised as follows

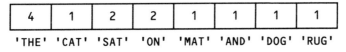

This table could become large, if the data file is large, but there will always be an element for each different word and within that element a number indicating how many times that word occurs.

5.4   Converting a Table to an Array

It is very easy to store information in tables, but in most cases that information cannot be accessed again easily because the values of the subscripts are not known to the programmer, as they have been picked up out of the data. In order to access the elements of a table one after another, the table must first be converted to an array. This is such a frequent requirement that SNOBOL provides a function CONVERT to do it.

The following statement converts a table T to an array called A

    A = CONVERT(T,'ARRAY')

The result of this statement is an array A of size n,2 where n is the number of elements in T which have non-null values. The array can be thought of as having two columns and as many rows as there were table elements. The element in the first column contains the table subscript and the element in the second column contains the contents of the corresponding table element. The elements can then be accessed by numeric pointers.

If the table created by the example given above was converted to an array, it could be visualised as follows

THE	4
CAT	1
SAT	2
ON	2
MAT	1
AND	1
DOG	1
RUG	1

remembering that the elements would still be in the random order in which they were stored in the table.

The conversion fails if there is nothing in the table. It is therefore advisable to test for failure when CONVERT is used, and to print an appropriate message if the table is empty. This is a common cause of error, particularly when a table is empty because a pattern has been used to find material to put in it and the pattern does not find what it is supposed to find.

A table may be converted to an array whose name is the same as the name of the table.

    DICT = CONVERT(DICT,'ARRAY')

In this case the table form of the information is lost.

    NEWDICT = CONVERT(DICT,'ARRAY')

keeps the table form of the information in DICT as well as converting it to the array form in NEWDICT.

Once the table has been converted to an array, its contents can be printed out or accessed systematically for further processing.

The program given above to store word counts in a table could continue

```
*
*   Print results
*
PRINT T = CONVERT(T,'ARRAY')          :F(EMPTY)
        I = 1
LOOP    OUTPUT = T<I,1> ' = ' T<I,2>   :F(END)
        I = I + 1                      :(LOOP)
*
*   Error message if table is empty
*
EMPTY OUTPUT = 'NO WORDS FOUND'
END
```

The output would be

```
THE = 4
CAT = 1
SAT = 2
ON = 2
MAT = 1
AND = 1
DOG = 1
RUG = 1
```

The variable I is the row subscript of the array and is thus used to point to successive pairs of words and counts. Column 1 holds the word and column 2 the count which corresponds to that word as is shown below.

Remember that the order in which the words are printed is random. They are neither in alphabetical order nor in the order in which they appear in the data. More program statements are required to print them in a more meaningful order. Some ways of doing this are described later in this book.

5.5 Use of Tables in Expanding Abbreviations

Another quite different use of tables is in expanding abbreviations. At the beginning of the program, a table element must be created for each abbreviation, using the abbreviation as the subscript and the full version as the contents.

If the following abbreviations were used

```
NY   New York
AM   Amsterdam
PA   Paris
MD   Madrid
RO   Rome
LN   London
```

a table `CITIES` would be set up as

```
CITIES = TABLE(6)
CITIES<'NY'> = 'New York'
CITIES<'AM'> = 'Amsterdam'
CITIES<'PA'> = 'Paris'
CITIES<'MD'> = 'Madrid'
CITIES<'RO'> = 'Rome'
CITIES<'LN'> = 'London'
```

If `PLACE` has successive values of `NY`, `AM`, `PA`, `MD`, `RO` and `LN` the statement

```
OUTPUT = CITIES<PLACE>
```

would print

```
New York
Amsterdam
Paris
Madrid
Rome
London
```

A single SNOBOL statement therefore does all that is necessary to search the table.

Note that the table subscripts are strings, not variables containing strings.

```
CITIES<NY>
```

would create an element of `CITIES` subscripted by the contents of `NY`. This table element would probably be empty.

Setting up the abbreviations can be laborious. They could be done in the following way.

```
     CITIES = TABLE(6)
     ABBREVS = 'NYAMPAMDROLN'
     FULL = 'New York/Amsterdam/Paris/Madrid/Rome/London/'
NEXT FULL BREAK('/') . CITY '/' =    :F(SET)
     ABBREVS LEN(2) . CODE =
     CITIES<CODE> = CITY              :(NEXT)
SET
```

The variable ABBREVS holds the abbreviations as a string. The individual abbreviations can be retrieved from ABBREVS because they each consist of two characters. The variable FULL holds the full names of the cities, separated by slashes. BREAK('/') can then be used to extract the cities. The statement

```
NEXT   FULL BREAK('/') . CITY '/' =  :F(SET)
```

extracts the first city, puts it in CITY and deletes it and the following slash from FULL.

```
       ABBREVS LEN(2) . CODE =
```

puts the first code in CODE and deletes it from ABBREVS. At this stage CITY contains New York and CODE contains NY.

```
       CITIES<CODE> = CITY
```

is therefore the equivalent of

```
       CITIES<'NY'> = 'New York'
```

The program loops back to NEXT to deal with the next pair and so on until BREAK('/') fails, indicating that there are no more cities left in FULL.

While this method of setting up abbreviations requires less typing it is less easy to see what the codes and corresponding full versions are or whether there is a mistake anywhere.

Another method is to read them in as data. This means that the program does not have to be altered if the abbreviations do. The following section of program sets up the same abbreviations, reading them as data which is in the form

```
NY New York
AM Amsterdam
PA Paris
```

etc.

```
       CITIES = TABLE(6)
NEXT   LINE = INPUT                        :F(READ)
       LINE LEN(2) . CODE LEN(1) REM . CITY
       CITIES<CODE> = CITY                 :(NEXT)
READ
```

In this case the input must be trimmed to ensure that there are no spaces on the end of the name of the city.

If the real data which the program is to analyse follows on after the abbreviations the program must be able to detect when it has reached the end of the abbreviations. This can be done by counting them, if the total number is known and is not likely to change. The following section of program deals with six

```
       CITIES = TABLE(6)
       I = 1
NEXT   LINE = INPUT                        :F(ERR)
       LINE LEN(2) . CODE LEN(1) REM . CITY
       CITIES<CODE> = CITY
       I = LT(I,6) I + 1                    :S(NEXT)F(READ)
ERR    OUTPUT = 'Error - not enough cities'    :(END)
READ
```

Note that the program includes an error message if there are insufficient cities in the data, i.e. less than six lines.

If the number of abbreviations is likely to vary, an extra line must be inserted at the end of them. The program detects the end when it reaches this line. If the extra line was

```
***ENDABBREVS
```

the program would be

```
      CITIES = TABLE()
NEXT  LINE = INPUT                          :F(ERR)
      LINE '***ENDABBREVS'                  :S(READ)
      LINE LEN(2) . CODE LEN(1) REM . CITY
      CITIES<CODE> = CITY                   :(NEXT)
ERR   OUTPUT = 'Error - end of cities not detected'      :(END)
READ
```

Again the program includes a test for input failure in case the line ***ENDABBREVS is inadvertently omitted from the data.

5   Example Programs

1.   This program counts the number of occurrences of words which begin with T. The counts are stored in the table COUNT which is converted to the array COUNT for printing. If the table is empty a message NO WORDS BEGINNING WITH "T" FOUND is printed.

```
*****************************************************************
*
*   Program to count the number of occurrences of words which
*   begin with T
*
*****************************************************************
*
*   Initialisation
*
      &STLIMIT = 10000
      &TRIM = 1
      &ANCHOR = 1
      LETTERS = 'ABCDEFGHIJKLMNOPQRSTUVWXYZ'
      WORDPAT = BREAK(LETTERS) SPAN(LETTERS) . WORD
      COUNT = TABLE()
*
*   Read a line
*
READ  LINE = INPUT                        :F(PRINT)
*
*   Count words
*
NEXT  LINE WORDPAT =                       :F(READ)
      WORD 'T'                             :F(NEXT)
      COUNT<WORD> = COUNT<WORD> + 1   :(NEXT)
```

```
*
*    Print results - first the heading
*
PRINT OUTPUT = 'WORD COUNT OF WORDS BEGINNING WITH "T"'
      OUTPUT =
*
*   then the words and counts
*
      COUNT = CONVERT(COUNT,'ARRAY')           :F(EMPTY)
      I = 1
AGAIN OUTPUT = COUNT<I,1> ' = ' COUNT<I,2>   :F(END)
      I = I + 1    :(AGAIN)
*
*  Error message if no words found
*
EMPTY OUTPUT = 'NO WORDS BEGINNING WITH "T" FOUND'
END
```

2.   This program shows the use of tables to expand abbreviations. It assumes that its data consists of paintings, one per line. The first two columns of each line contain an identification number. Columns 8 and 9 contain a code indicating the artist. The following codes are used

```
RA    Raphael
TI    Titian
TT    Tintoretto
TP    Tiepolo
EG    El Greco
VL    Velazquez
MR    Murillo
GY    Goya
```

The painting's title is the last item on the line and starts in column 25.

The program prints out the identification number, the full name of the artist and the title of the painting.

```
***************************************************************
*
*   Program to print titles of paintings and full names
*   of artists
*
***************************************************************
*
*   Initialisation
*
      &STLIMIT = 10000
      &ANCHOR = 1
      &TRIM = 1
*
*   Set up table of artists
*
      ARTISTS = TABLE(8)
      ARTISTS<'RA'> = 'Raphael'
      ARTISTS<'TI'> = 'Titian'
```

```
        ARTISTS<'TT'> = 'Tintoretto'
        ARTISTS<'TP'> = 'Tiepolo'
        ARTISTS<'EG'> = 'El Greco'
        ARTISTS<'VL'> = 'Velazquez'
        ARTISTS<'MR'> = 'Murillo'
        ARTISTS<'GY'> = 'Goya'
*
*  Set up pattern to extract fields from data
*
        BREAKUP = LEN(2) . IDEN LEN(5) LEN(2) . ARTIST LEN(15)
+ REM . TITLE
*
*  Print heading followed by a blank line
*
        OUTPUT = DUPL(' ',4) 'Iden Artist' DUPL(' ',10)
+ 'Title'
        OUTPUT =
*
*  Read a line and extract fields from it
*
MORE   LINE = INPUT    :F(END)
        LINE BREAKUP
*
*  Output required fields
*
        OUTPUT = DUPL(' ',6) IDEN ' ' ARTISTS<ARTIST>
+ DUPL(' ',16 - SIZE(ARTISTS<ARTIST>)) TITLE    :(MORE)
END
```

DUPL is used to calculate how many spaces are to be printed after the name of the artist so that the titles are lined up in a column. The width of the column allowed for the name is sixteen characters. Therefore 16 − SIZE(ARTISTS<ARTIST>) is the number of spaces required to fill it out.

If the first three lines of data were

```
1*****TI***************Adam and Eve
2*****EG***************Adoration of the Shepherds
3*****GY***************The Flower Garden
```

using * for unwanted information, the program would print

```
    Iden Artist         Title

       1 Titian          Adam and Eve
       2 El Greco        Adoration of the Shepherds
       3 Goya            The Flower Garden
```

5 Exercises

5.1   Make a word count of all words in the sonnet which begin with R, S or T. Print them out together with their frequencies.

5.2   Count the number of people from each occupation.

5.3   Modify 5.2 so that the full names of the occupations are printed.

5.4   For each person in the people file, print out the identification number, name and date of birth. Write the dates with the names of the months so that e.g. 18900621 appears as 21 June 1890.

6 User-Defined Functions

6.1 Organising a Program

So far the programs we have looked at have been short, or at least short enough for the programmer to consider all of the program at the same time. When a larger program is being written, it is necessary to break the program down into smaller processes, each of which can be considered to be a separate piece of program.

Any of the separate pieces of program may be required in several different places in the program, using different variables although the same process is performed on them. Like other programming languages, SNOBOL provides a mechanism for writing these statements once and then calling them into use whenever they are required. Such sets of statements are called user-defined functions in SNOBOL and once they have been defined, they can be used in the same way as the built-in functions.

6.1.1 A Program Needing a Function

The following program shows what happens when three tables are to be printed and the programmer does not use a function to do the printing. The statements which print each table are identical except for the name of the table, the labels and the number which is used in the messages.

```
****************************************************************
*
*   This is a bad program which should not be imitated
*   It is intended to show why functions are necessary
*
*   Program to count words of 3, 4 and 5 letters
*
****************************************************************
*
*   Initialisation
*
        &STLIMIT = 10000
        &ANCHOR = 1
        &TRIM = 1
        LETTERS = 'ABCDEFGHIJKLMNOPQRSTUVWXYZ'
        WORDPAT = BREAK(LETTERS) SPAN(LETTERS) . WORD
        LET3 = TABLE()
        LET4 = TABLE()
        LET5 = TABLE()
*
*   Read a line
*
READ    LINE = INPUT          :F(PRINT)
*
```

```
*   Count words with 3 letters, 4 letters and 5 letters in
*   separate tables
*
NEXT  LINE WORDPAT =            :F(READ)
      EQ(SIZE(WORD),3)         :S(ADD.1)
      EQ(SIZE(WORD),4)         :S(ADD.2)
      NE(SIZE(WORD),5)         :S(NEXT)
      LET5<WORD> = LET5<WORD> + 1     :(NEXT)
ADD.1 LET3<WORD> = LET3<WORD> + 1     :(NEXT)
ADD.2 LET4<WORD> = LET4<WORD> + 1     :(NEXT)
*
*   Print results
*   Firstly table of 3 letter words
*
PRINT OUTPUT = 'Table of words with 3 letters'
      OUTPUT =
      LET3 = CONVERT(LET3,'ARRAY')           :F(ERR.1)
      I = 1
OUT.1 OUTPUT = LET3<I,1> ' ' LET3<I,2>       :F(PR.1)
      I = I + 1          :(OUT.1)
*
*   Error message if no 3 letter words found
*
ERR.1  OUTPUT = 'No words with 3 letters found'
*
*   Print table of 4 letter words
*
PR.1  OUTPUT =
      OUTPUT =
      OUTPUT = 'Table of words with 4 letters'
      OUTPUT =
      LET4 = CONVERT(LET4,'ARRAY')           :F(ERR.2)
      I = 1
OUT.2 OUTPUT = LET4<I,1> ' ' LET4<I,2>       :F(PR.2)
      I = I + 1          :(OUT.2)
*
*   Error message if no 4 letter words found
*
ERR.2 OUTPUT = 'No words with 4 letters found'
*
*   Print table of 5 letter words
*
PR.2  OUTPUT =
      OUTPUT =
      OUTPUT = 'Table of words with 5 letters'
      OUTPUT =
      LET5 = CONVERT(LET5,'ARRAY')           :F(ERR.3)
      I = 1
OUT.3 OUTPUT = LET5<I,1> ' ' LET5<I,2>       :F(END)
      I = I + 1          :(OUT.3)
*
*   Error message if no 5 letter words found
*
ERR.3 OUTPUT = 'No words with 5 letters found'
END
```

A better way to organise this program would be to write the printing statements once only as a function and then call them into use when they are required.

6.2   Outline of a Program with a Function

In a program which uses a user-defined function there are three separate references to the function.

1.   The function definition which declares the name of the function.
2.   Calls or uses of the function.
3.   The function code, i.e. statements which carry out the process required.

A program which uses a function can be represented schematically:

```
function definition
        .
        .
        .
main program
 including
call(s) of function
        .
        .
function code
```

There may be many functions in a program, but each function should have the three items mentioned above.

6.3   Calling a Function

A user-defined function is used or 'called' in much the same way as a built-in function. The function normally has one or more arguments and is called by giving the function name followed by the names of the arguments in brackets.

The number of arguments to a function depends on what the programmer requires the function to do. For example,

```
PRINT(WORDS)
```

could print a table called WORDS.

```
PRINT(T)
```

could print a table called T.

If the programmer required the function to print a table with a message containing a number which varied with each call of the function, two arguments would be needed. For example,

```
PRINT(WORDS,3)
```

might print a table called WORDS with 3 as the number.

Another call could be

```
PRINT(T,5)
```

to print a table T with the number 5 in the messages.

6.4 Function Code

The lines of program, which make up the function, are called the function code and may be placed anywhere in a program. They can be identified because the first line of the function code has a label which is normally the same as the name of the function. This is known as the entry label. For example, the function code of a function called PRINT would begin with an entry label PRINT.

It is best to write the function code separately from the rest of the program and to think of it as an independent unit of code.

6.4.1 Position of the Function Code within the Program

The function code is best placed at the end of the program. It must only be executed when the function is called. The calling statements are elsewhere in the program.

The program must not be allowed to flow down into the function. The statement before the function code must therefore have an unconditional goto or a conditional goto with two branches, as is shown in the following diagram.

```
function definition
      .
      .
main program
 including
calling statement(s)
      .
      .                          :(   )
      .
function code
```

An alternative is to place the function code immediately after the function definition. In this case there must be a jump round the function code after the definition statement to ensure that the function code is only executed when it is called.

```
      function definition       :(HERE)
      function code
            .
            .
            .
HERE  start of main program
            .
            .
      calling statement(s)
            .
            .
            .
```

6.4.2   Function Arguments

The function code is written using fictitious or dummy variables. The names of the real variables on which it is to operate (i.e. the arguments) are given when the function is called and are substituted for the dummy ones when the function is being executed.

6.4.3   Missing Arguments

One or more arguments may be missing. For example, a function which normally has three arguments may have only two arguments in a particular call. In this case the function code must recognise this and make an assumption for what is required. In computer terms, this is called the *default*. If a function which had been defined with two arguments was called as

```
PRINT(WORDS)
```

with the second argument missing, the function could make an assumption for the second argument. Within the function code this can be done as follows

```
N = IDENT(N) 3
```

which sets N to 3 if N is null. A missing argument is treated as null if it is not set within the function code. If the missing arguments are not the last ones, the comma which separates them must still be given in the function call.

For a function defined with three arguments, the second argument is missing in a call of

```
PRINT(WORDS,,'Forward Order')
```

6.4.4   Local Variables

A function may need one or more variables which are in use only when the function is being executed and are not required elsewhere in the program. These are called local variables. One example would be the pointer I which is used when the array in the program given in Section 6.1.1 is being printed, but is not used elsewhere in the program.

6.4.5   Labels within a Function

When writing the code of a function, it is advisable to use labels which begin with the name of the function. This prevents confusion between labels within a function and those in the main part of the program. In SNOBOL all labels are global, i.e. they are accessible from anywhere in a program, either within a function or the main part. This means that it is possible to jump from the main part of a program into the middle of a function, but the result is likely to be nonsense. Function code should only be accessed when it is called, not by jumping into the middle of it. Using labels which begin with the name of the function within the function helps to eliminate this problem and also prevents duplicate labels appearing within a program. It is also good practice to terminate a function with a null statement consisting of the name of the function plus .END.

The printing function could end with

```
PRINT.END
```

6.4.6 Getting Out of a Function

When the function has completed its task the program must go back to the statement which called the function and carry on what it was doing there. This is done by using a special label RETURN after a goto in the function. There is no real label RETURN in the program. It simply means go back to the statement which called the function and carry on from there.

6.5 Function Definition

The arguments and any local variables used by a function are declared by the built-in function DEFINE which also gives the function its name. The arguments are declared using the dummy variable names which are used in the function code. When a function is called, the arguments are substituted by position, the first real variable for the first dummy one, the second real variable for the second dummy one and so on.

To declare a function PRINT with one argument DICT (the table to be printed) and no local variables

```
DEFINE('PRINT(DICT)')
```

Note how the apostrophes are used. PRINT(DICT) is a string which gives the general form of a call of the function. It is called the prototype.

If the function had a local variable I, the function definition would be written as

```
DEFINE('PRINT(DICT)I')
```

For two arguments, DICT and N, and two local variables I and J, the definition would be

```
DEFINE('PRINT(DICT,N)I,J')
```

The function definition statement should be given as one of the initialisation statements at the beginning of the program, to avoid the possibility of the program calling a function which has not been defined.

It is possible to have a function which has no arguments. The brackets must still be given in the definition as in

```
DEFINE('PRINT()')
```

An entry label which is different from the name of the function may be used. In this case the entry label must also be given on the function definition. The following definition of PRINT gives an entry label STARTP.

```
DEFINE('PRINT(DICT,N)I','STARTP')
```

6.6 Example of a Program with a Function

The program in Section 6.1.1 could be rewritten as follows with a function.

```
*********************************************************************
*
*   Program to count the occurrences of all 3 letter, 4 letter
*   and 5 letter words
*
*   It uses a function PRINT to print the tables
*
*********************************************************************
*
*   Initialisation
*
        &STLIMIT = 10000
        &ANCHOR = 1
        &TRIM = 1
        LETTERS = 'ABCDEFGHIJKLMNOPQRSTUVWXYZ'
        WORDPAT = BREAK(LETTERS) SPAN(LETTERS) . WORD
        LET3 = TABLE()
        LET4 = TABLE()
        LET5 = TABLE()
        DEFINE('PRINT(LIST,N)I')
*
*   Read a line
*
READ    LINE = INPUT               :F(RES)
*
*   Count words with 3 letters, 4 letters and 5 letters in
*   separate tables
*
NEXT    LINE WORDPAT =             :F(READ)
        EQ(SIZE(WORD),3)           :S(ADD.1)
        EQ(SIZE(WORD),4)           :S(ADD.2)
        NE(SIZE(WORD),5)           :S(NEXT)
        LET5<WORD> = LET5<WORD> + 1      :(NEXT)
ADD.1   LET3<WORD> = LET3<WORD> + 1      :(NEXT)
ADD.2   LET4<WORD> = LET4<WORD> + 1      :(NEXT)
*
*   Print results
*   calling function PRINT for each table
*
RES     PRINT(LET3,3)
        PRINT(LET4,4)
        PRINT(LET5,5)                    :(END)
*
*   Code for function PRINT(LIST,N)
*
*   Prints a table LIST - N is a value used in the headings
*
PRINT     OUTPUT =
          OUTPUT =
          OUTPUT = 'Table of words with ' N ' letters'
          OUTPUT =
          LIST = CONVERT(LIST,'ARRAY')       :F(PRINT.2)
          I = 1
PRINT.1   OUTPUT = LIST<I,1> '  ' LIST<I,2>    :F(RETURN)
          I = I + 1                          :(PRINT.1)
```

```
*
*  Error message if no words found
*
PRINT.2  OUTPUT = 'No words with ' N ' letters found'
+      :(RETURN)
PRINT.END
END
```

The function definition statement

```
DEFINE('PRINT(LIST,N)I')
```

declares two arguments LIST and N. The function is actually called three times by the following statements

```
PRINT(LET3,3)
PRINT(LET4,4)
PRINT(LET5,5)
```

The first time that it is called the program goes to the label PRINT, substituting LET3 for LIST and 3 for N. It continues from the label PRINT until the statement labelled PRINT.1 fails, indicating that the end of the array has been reached. The goto :F(RETURN) sends the program back to the calling statement PRINT(LET3,3) and the program continues from there. In this case the next statement is another call of PRINT, this time for table LET4 with the number 4 as the second argument. After executing the statements within PRINT, it returns to the calling statement and finds that the next statement again calls up PRINT, this time for the five letter table. After returning again from PRINT, the remainder of the calling statement :(END) is executed, ensuring that the program does not flow down into PRINT, but jumps round it to terminate at END.

6.7 Local and Global Variables

The names of variables declared on a function definition statement are local to that function and these variables can be ignored when the program is not in the function. This means that a program can use the same name inside and outside a function to refer to two different variables. This applies also to the dummy arguments. When a function is called, a copy of each real argument is made into the corresponding dummy argument. If the contents of the arguments are altered within the function, they remain unchanged outside it, and their value on exit from the function is the same as that on entry.

Variables can appear in the main part of a program and within a function. These are called global variables. They are not declared on the function definition statement and their values can be altered by the function. However, this practice is not recommended as it makes the function specific to one particular program. Variables which are required to be altered within a function are best passed to the function by name (Section 7.7).

6.8 Functions Which Return a Value

A user-defined function can return a value, that is a number or string which it has computed from its arguments. A function which returns a value must return with the value it has computed in a variable whose name is the same as the name of the function.

The following example gives the definition and code of a function COUNT which counts the number of times its first string argument WORD occurs in its second string argument TEXT. For ease of understanding a simple pattern using the unanchored mode is used.

```
        &ANCHOR = 0
        DEFINE('COUNT(WORD,TEXT)')
                    .
                    .
                    .
        main program
                    .
                    .
                    .
*
*   Function COUNT(WORD,TEXT) returns the
*   number of times that WORD occurs in TEXT
*
COUNT    COUNT = 0
COUNT.1 TEXT WORD =              :F(RETURN)
         COUNT = COUNT + 1       :(COUNT.1)
COUNT.END
```

When the statement

```
COUNT.1 TEXT WORD =              :F(RETURN)
```

fails the variable COUNT contains the number which has been computed.

This function is called in the same way as built-in functions which return a value.

To count how many times VOWEL occurs in WORDS and assign the result to TOTAL

```
        TOTAL = COUNT(VOWEL,WORDS)
```

To add the number of times which LETTERS occurs in SENT to LCOUNT

```
        LCOUNT = COUNT(LETTERS,SENT) + LCOUNT
```

A very simple but complete program using this function counts the number of occurrences of AE and AI in its data.

```
***********************************************************************
*
*   Program to count the number of occurrences of AE and AI
*   in its data
*
***********************************************************************
```

```
*
*   Initialisation
*
        &TRIM = 1
        &STLIMIT = 10000
        &ANCHOR = 0
        DEFINE('COUNT(WORD,TEXT)')
*
*   Main program
*
MORE    LINE = INPUT                           :F(PRINT)
        ACOUNT = COUNT('AE',LINE) + ACOUNT
        ICOUNT = COUNT('AI',LINE) + ICOUNT   :(MORE)
*
*   Print results
*
PRINT OUTPUT = 'NO. OF OCCURRENCES OF "AE" IS ' ACOUNT
        OUTPUT = 'NO. OF OCCURRENCES OF "AI" IS ' ICOUNT   :(END)
*
*   Function COUNT(WORD,TEXT) returns the
*   number of times that WORD occurs in TEXT
*
COUNT    COUNT =
COUNT.1 TEXT WORD =                 :F(RETURN)
        COUNT = COUNT + 1    :(COUNT.1)
COUNT.END
END
```

The function COUNT is called twice after each line has been input. The goto :(END) ensures that the program jumps round the function code to terminate correctly, once it has printed the results.

6.9   Functions Which Ask a Question

User-defined functions may ask a question and therefore need to return indicating succeed or fail. The goto :(RETURN) returns indicating success. :(FRETURN) returns indicating failure. The success or failure of the function is detected by the calling statement in the main program.

The function BEGIN detects whether the first N letters of its two string arguments are identical.

```
        DEFINE('BEGIN(TEXT1,TEXT2,N)CH1,CH2')
                .
                .
        main program
                .
                .
*
*   Function BEGIN(TEXT1,TEXT2,N) tests whether the
*   first N letters of TEXT1 and TEXT2 are
*   identical
```

```
*
BEGIN TEXT1 LEN(N) . CH1
      TEXT2 LEN(N) . CH2
      IDENT(CH1,CH2)              :S(RETURN)F(FRETURN)
BEGIN.END
```

The following program uses the BEGIN function to test whether the first two or first three letters of words are identical. For the sake of simplicity, each pair of words to be compared is read on one line. The two words on each line are separated by a slash. A count of words which have three and two letters identical is kept in COUNT3 and COUNT2 respectively.

```
******************************************************************
*
*   Program to test whether the first three or first
*   two letters of words are identical
*
******************************************************************
*
*   Initialisation
*
      &TRIM = 1
      &ANCHOR = 1
      &STLIMIT = 10000
      DEFINE('BEGIN(TEXT1,TEXT2,N)CH1,CH2')      :(MORE)
*
*   Function BEGIN(TEXT1,TEXT2,N) tests whether the
*   first N letters of TEXT1 and TEXT2 are
*   identical
*
BEGIN TEXT1 LEN(N) . CH1
      TEXT2 LEN(N) . CH2
      IDENT(CH1,CH2)              :S(RETURN)F(FRETURN)
BEGIN.END
*
*   Read words
*
MORE  LINE = INPUT               :F(PRINT)
      LINE BREAK('/') . WORD1 '/' REM . WORD2
*
*   Compare first three letters
*
      BEGIN(WORD1,WORD2,3)       :F(TWO)
*
*   Success - count and get next pair
*
      COUNT3 = COUNT3 + 1        :(MORE)
*
*   Compare first two letters
*
TWO   BEGIN(WORD1,WORD2,2)       :F(MORE)
*
* Success  - count and get next pair
*
      COUNT2 = COUNT2 + 1        :(MORE)
```

```
*
* Print totals
*
PRINT OUTPUT = 'Number of words with first three letters '
+  'identical is ' COUNT3
       OUTPUT = 'Number of words with first two letters '
+  'identical is ' COUNT2
END
```

In this program the code for the function BEGIN is placed immediately after the function definition statement. This is another possible place for it. The program jumps to MORE after the definition so that the function code is only executed when it is called from further on in the program. For each pair of words, BEGIN is called first to test the first three letters. If this fails, it is called a second time to test the first two letters.

6.10   User-Defined Pattern Functions

User-defined pattern functions may also be written. In the following example the function SKIPOVER(S) matches the first occurrence of the characters in S with any one character between each of the characters in S. SKIPOVER('AE') matches AME in CAME, AXE, ADE in LEMONADE, etc.

```
        DEFINE('SKIPOVER(S)CH')
                 .
                 .
        main program
                 .
                 .
                 .
*
*  Function SKIPOVER(S) matches a string which is the same as S
*  but with one character between each of the characters in S
*
SKIPOVER
            SKIPOVER =
*
*  Do not add an extra character after the last character in S
*
SKIPOVER.1   EQ(SIZE(S),1)     :S(SKIPOVER.2)
*
*  Take a character from S and put it in SKIPOVER followed
*  by LEN(1) to represent any one character
*
            S LEN(1) . CH   =
            SKIPOVER = SKIPOVER CH LEN(1)        :(SKIPOVER.1)
*
*  Special case for last character
*
SKIPOVER.2   SKIPOVER = SKIPOVER S      :(RETURN)
SKIPOVER.END
```

The function is used in the following program which finds words which have S, A and E as first, third and fifth characters or L and S as first and third characters.

```
********************************************************************
*
*   Program to find words which match S*A*E or L*S
*   where * is any character
*
********************************************************************
*
* Initialisation
*
        &TRIM = 1
        &ANCHOR = 1
        &STLIMIT = 10000
        DEFINE('SKIPOVER(S)CH')
        LETTERS = 'ABCDEFGHIJKLMNOPQRSTUVWXYZ'
        WORDPAT = BREAK(LETTERS) SPAN(LETTERS) . WORD
*
*   The pattern PAT uses the function SKIPOVER
*
        PAT = SKIPOVER('SAE') | SKIPOVER('LS')
*
*   Read a line
*
MORE LINE = INPUT               :F(END)
*
*   Get a word from LINE and test it against PAT
*
AGAIN LINE WORDPAT =            :F(MORE)
        WORD PAT                :F(AGAIN)
*
*   Print the word if successful
*
        OUTPUT = WORD           :(AGAIN)
*
*   Function SKIPOVER(S) matches a string which is the same as S
*   but with one character between each of the characters in S
*
SKIPOVER
            SKIPOVER =
*
*   Do not add an extra character after the last character in S
*
SKIPOVER.1  EQ(SIZE(S),1)       :S(SKIPOVER.2)
*
*   Take a character from S and put it in SKIPOVER followed
*   by LEN(1) to represent any one character
*
            S LEN(1) . CH   =
            SKIPOVER = SKIPOVER CH LEN(1)           :(SKIPOVER.1)
*
*   Special case for last character
*
SKIPOVER.2  SKIPOVER = SKIPOVER S       :(RETURN)
SKIPOVER.END
END
```

6.11   Writing Larger Programs

Larger programs should be thought of as a collection of functions. The functions should be written so that each is almost an independent unit of code. Once a set of functions has been written, they may be used over and over again in different programs. It is easiest if each function can be thought of first only in terms of its definition. Once the programmer decides that PRINT(DICT) prints a table, calls to PRINT can be placed in a program without the need to think about the function code for PRINT, which can be written separately.

User-defined functions may call other user-defined functions as well as built-in functions. They may also call themselves. These are known as recursive functions.

6   Exercises

6.1   Make a frequency count of all words in the sonnet which begin with a vowel and all those which end with a vowel using a function to print the tables.

6.2   Write a program to validate the people data, checking that only valid codes appear for the place of birth and occupation and that only valid characters appear in the names.

7 More Operators

7.1 Operators

Besides the arithmetic operators of + - * and /, SNOBOL has other symbols which act as operators on one or more variables. The arithmetic operators are binary operators in that they link two variables or objects. For example, in

```
X = Y + Z
```

the + operates on both Y and Z. There must always be at least one space on either side of a binary operator. Other examples of binary operators which we have seen so far are = and the full stop used in conditional value assignment.

A unary operator operates on only one variable which is called its *operand*. There is no space between the operator and its operand. The same symbol can be used both as a binary and as a unary operand and has a different meaning for each. SNOBOL uses the spacing or lack of it between the operator and the following variable to determine which use of the operator is intended.

7.2 Cursor Position Operator

The unary operator @ can be used in a pattern to assign the current cursor position as an integer value to a variable.

After

```
&ANCHOR = 0
TEXT = 'SNOBOL'
TEXT 'O' @X
```

X has the value 3 as the cursor is positioned between the first O and the B of SNOBOL, i.e. between the third and the fourth characters.

The position of the cursor position operator and its associated variable within the pattern is important. After the statement

```
TEXT @X 'O'
```

X has the value 2, as @X is before the O in the pattern.

After

```
TEXT BREAK('O') @X
```

X has the value 2 as the cursor is again positioned before the O.

The cursor position operator may be used more than once in a pattern, normally with a different variable each time. It may also be used in conjunction with the other pattern match operators.

```
TEXT = 'SNOBOL'
TEXT BREAK('O') . V1 @X BREAK('L') . V2 @Y
```

After this V1 contains SN, V2 contains OBO, X has the value 2 and Y the value 5.

7.3 Immediate Value Assignment

In a conditional value assignment (Section 2.9) the full stop operator only makes an assignment if the entire pattern matches. This is in contrast with immediate value assignment, where the binary operator $ assigns a value to a variable if the associated component of a pattern matches regardless of whether the whole pattern matches. Immediate value assignment could be used, for example, in a large pattern to find out how much of it was matched successfully or to observe the behaviour of the pattern on test data. This can be seen in

```
WORD = 'HIDDEN'
    PAT = ('H' | 'HI') $ OUTPUT ('I' | 'ID') $ OUTPUT
+ ('E' | 'EN') $ OUTPUT
    WORD PAT
```

where the following lines are printed before the pattern match fails.

```
H
I
ID
HI
```

The pattern first matches the H of the first pair of alternatives. It then moves to the second pair of alternatives and matches the first of these, the I. It moves next to the third pair of alternatives and finds that neither of them matches and so backtracks to the second pair and obtains a match with the second alternative, ID. Again the third pair does not yield a match and so the pattern backtracks to the first pair and matches HI. This time, the second pair does not match at all. If &ANCHOR is 1, the pattern fails at this point. If &ANCHOR is 0, the pattern attempts to match again, beginning at the second character of the pattern subject and then at the third character and so on until there are insufficient characters left. In this example the attempts from the second character onwards fail because there are no more occurrences of H in the pattern subject.

In

```
&ANCHOR = 0
TEXT = 'CATS AND DOGS'
VOWELPAT = ANY('AEIOU') $ V 'S'
```

first the A in CAT is matched and assigned to V. The S does not match because S is not the character immediately following A. (See Section 2.6.) However, the pattern makes further attempts to match, as &ANCHOR is set to 0. The second vowel, the A in AND, is assigned to V. Again N does not match so the next vowel, the O in DOGS is matched.

That is assigned to V. Still the S does not match, but the statement finishes with the value 0 in V.

7.4   Unevaluated Expressions

The unary operator * (as opposed to the arithmetic binary operator *) postpones the evaluation of its operand until that value is required during pattern matching. It enables a pattern to be constructed at the beginning of a program, when the value of an argument to a pattern function used within the pattern has not yet been assigned.

In the following statement

```
PAT = LEN(6) . FIRST
```

a pattern is defined which assigns the first 6 characters to FIRST. If a more general form of the pattern is required to assign the first N characters to FIRST, the pattern definition

```
PAT = LEN(N) . FIRST
```

would not be possible because it would use whatever value was in N before the pattern was defined. In most circumstances, this would be null. Therefore a new value of N could not be used during execution.

If the pattern is defined as an unevaluated expression

```
PAT = LEN(*N) . FIRST
```

every time that the pattern is used, the current value of N is taken as the argument to LEN. In

```
        &ANCHOR = 1
        PAT = LEN(*N) . FIRST
MORE    LINE = INPUT
        LINE SPAN('0123456789') . N =
        LINE PAT              :(MORE)
```

the statement

```
LINE SPAN('0123456789') . N =
```

extracts a number from the beginning of LINE and assigns that number to N. This is then taken as the value of N when the pattern is executed in

```
LINE PAT              :(MORE)
```

7.5   Uses of Pattern Operators

Used in conjunction with the other pattern features described in this chapter, the unevaluated expression facility is very powerful. In the pattern definition

```
PAT = LEN(1) $ CH BREAK(*CH)
```

the value of CH in BREAK(*CH) is whatever is assigned to it by the first pattern element LEN(1) $ CH. Immediate value assignment after LEN(1) is necessary because the assignment must be made in order to evaluate the rest of the pattern. With &ANCHOR set to 0, this pattern matches any string in which any character is repeated. If &ANCHOR was 1 it would match any string in which the first character is repeated with any number of intervening characters.

If the pattern was defined as

```
PAT = LEN(1) $ CH BREAK(CH)
```

the value of CH in BREAK(CH) would be whatever was in CH before the pattern was defined, most probably nothing. When the pattern is used, BREAK(CH) would use that value, not the value of CH assigned by LEN(1) $ CH.

The pattern

```
PAT = LEN(1) $ V *V
```

matches the first occurrence of a letter immediately followed by itself. The &ANCHOR must be 0 for this pattern to succeed other than where the two letters occur at the beginning of a string.

A pattern which includes the cursor position operator and an unevaluated expression can be used to extract words from a line without deleting those words which have already been dealt with.

```
LETTERS = 'ABCDEFGHIJKLMNOPQRSTUVWXYZ'
PAT = TAB(*K) BREAK(LETTERS) SPAN(LETTERS) . WORD @K
```

The cursor position operator is used to record the position in LINE where the current word ends. When the pattern is next used, TAB(*K) moves to that position and BREAK(LETTERS) starts to look from there. K must be set to 0 for each new line of data.

7.6 Indirect Referencing

It is possible to treat the literal characters which are the contents of a variable as the name of another variable. This is called indirect referencing and the dollar sign ($) is used as its operator. In this case the dollar sign is a unary operator and there is no space between it and the variable which is its operand.

The following three statements print SNOBOL

```
WORD = 'SNOBOL'
TEXT = 'WORD'
OUTPUT = $TEXT
```

Here WORD is a string which is the contents of TEXT. The same string is also used as the name of a variable whose contents is SNOBOL. A further item can be added

```
WORD = 'SNOBOL'
SNOBOL = 'PROGRAM'
TEXT = 'WORD'
OUTPUT = $$TEXT
```

then prints PROGRAM.

In Chapter 1 it was seen that names of variables consist only of letters, numbers and full stops. This rule in fact applies only to names which appear explicitly in the program. Names can contain any characters other than letters, numbers and full stops, but indirect referencing must be used to access them.

```
$'DATA-1774' = INPUT
```

assigns the current input line to a variable called DATA-1774. The variable must always be referred to as $'DATA-1774', never DATA-1774.

```
$NEXT = INPUT
```

reads the next input line and assigns it to a variable whose name is the input string. If the input was 23 – 132, a variable with the name 23 – 132 would be created to hold the data.

7.6.1   Indirect Reference in Gotos

Indirect referencing can also be used in a goto field to compute the label. This allows multiple choices rather than the two which are available in an ordinary conditional goto.

If a program contained labels PRINT.REV, PRINT.FORW, PRINT.FREQ the label

```
:($('PRINT.' TYPE))
```

would go to PRINT.REV if TYPE contained REV, to PRINT.FORW if TYPE contained FORW and PRINT.FREQ if TYPE contained FREQ.

7.7   Name Operator

In Section 6.7 we saw that if the contents of function arguments are altered within the function, they remain unchanged outside it, that is, their value on exit from the function is the same as that on entry. A simple way of changing the contents of a variable within a function is to make that variable global, but this is not recommended because the function can only handle that one specific variable, not any variable. The function could not then be used in any other program.

Indirect reference on the function argument within a function is used to make the function handle any variable. The following function increments the value of whatever variable is its argument.

```
DEFINE('INCR(N)')
        .
        .
        .
INCR    $N = $N + 1          :(RETURN)
```

The name operator, a unary dot, must be used when the function is called.

```
INCR(.I)
```

increments the value of I. The dot ensures that the name of the variable is passed to the function. $N then refers to that variable. Without the dot, the contents of I would be passed to the function. If this happened and I contained 2, $N would refer to a variable whose name was 2. For a function

```
DEFINE('INCR(N)') ⌐
        .
        .
INCR  N = N + 1              :(RETURN)
```

and a call of

```
INCR(I)
```

the new value of I would not be passed back to the main program.

There are other circumstances where a unary dot is needed. (See Sections 8.4, 9.3.4 and 10.2.)

7 Example Programs

1. This program prints out all lines on which the first character is repeated.

```
***********************************************************************
*
*  Program to print out all lines on which
*  the first character is repeated
*
***********************************************************************
*
*  Initialisation
*
      &STLIMIT = 10000
      &TRIM = 1
      &ANCHOR = 1
      PAT = LEN(1) $ CH BREAK(*CH)
*
*  Read a line and test pattern against it
*
MORE  LINE = INPUT    :F(END)
      LINE PAT        :F(MORE)
      OUTPUT = LINE   :(MORE)
END
```

The pattern is constructed outside the loop but the value of CH is not known until the pattern match begins. Immediate value assignment is necessary because the assignment must be made in order to evaluate BREAK(*CH).

2. This program underlines the first instance of a doubled letter in each line of data. The pattern DOUBLE uses an unevaluated expression to find a doubled letter and the cursor position operator to determine where to print -- (the underlining characters).

```
******************************************************************
*
*  Program to underline the first instance of
*  a doubled letter in each line of data
*
******************************************************************
*
*  Initialisation
*
       &STLIMIT = 10000
       &TRIM = 1
       &ANCHOR = 0
       DOUBLE = LEN(1) $ V @X *V
*
* Read a line and print it
*
MORE   LINE = INPUT        :F(END)
       OUTPUT = LINE
*
*  Test double pattern and print
*  underlinings if successful
*
       LINE DOUBLE         :F(BL)
       OUTPUT = DUPL(' ',X - 1) '--'
BL     OUTPUT =            :(MORE)
END
```

3. This program prints out all lines which contain a word beginning with T, underlining the words beginning with T.

```
******************************************************************
*
*  Program to underline words which begin with T
*
******************************************************************
*
*  Initialisation
*
       &ANCHOR = 1
       &STLIMIT = 10000
       &TRIM = 1
       LETTERS = 'ABCDEFGHIJKLMNOPQRSTUVWXYZ'
       PAT = TAB(*K) @L BREAK(LETTERS) @M SPAN(LETTERS) . WORD @K
*
*  Read data and reset for a new line
*
MORE   LINE = INPUT              :F(END)
       K = 0
       PRINT = 'NO'
*
*  Look for words beginning with T
*
AGAIN  LINE PAT                  :F(PRINT)
       WORD 'T'                  :S(FOUND)
       PRINTCH = ' '             :(MAKE)
```

```
*
*  Set underlining character.
*  Print LINE once one word beginning with T is found in it
*
FOUND  OUTPUT = DIFFER(PRINT,'YES') LINE    :F(ADD)
       PRINT = 'YES'
ADD    PRINTCH = '-'
MAKE   UNDER = UNDER DUPL(' ',M - L) DUPL(PRINTCH,K - M) :(AGAIN)
*
*  Print underlinings
*
PRINT  OUTPUT = IDENT(PRINT,'YES') UNDER
       UNDER =             :(MORE)
END
```

The cursor position operator is used in the pattern PAT to set K to the position reached at the end of the current word. L is the position at the end of the previous word. M is the position at the beginning of the current word. M - L is the number of spaces in UNDER to cover the gap between words. One space is not enough because there may be punctuation. K - M is the number of characters required to underline the word.

The underlining character PRINTCH is set to a minus sign whenever a word beginning with T is found. Otherwise it is a space. The appropriate combination of minus signs and spaces is built up in UNDER which is printed when all the words in a line have been dealt with.

The line is only printed once even though there may be several words beginning with T in it. PRINT is set to YES once the line is printed. The statement

```
FOUND  OUTPUT = DIFFER(PRINT,'YES') LINE    :F(ADD)
```

only prints the line if PRINT does not contain YES. PRINT has to be set back to NO for each new line.

4. This program counts the occurrences of all words with 1 to 8 letters using a different table for each number of letters. It uses indirect referencing to construct the names of the tables from the string 'LET' and the number of letters.

```
*****************************************************************
*
*  This program counts the occurrences of all words with 1 to 8
*  letters using a table for each number of letters
*
*  Indirect referencing is used to construct the names of the
*  tables from the string 'LET' and the number of letters
*
*****************************************************************
*
*  Initialisation
*
       &STLIMIT = 10000
       &ANCHOR = 1
       &TRIM = 1
       LETTERS = 'ABCDEFGHIJKLMNOPQRSTUVWXYZ'
       WORDPAT = BREAK(LETTERS) SPAN(LETTERS) . WORD
```

```
*
*   Construct table names
*
      M = 1
NEXT  $('LET' M) = TABLE()
      M = LT(M,8) M + 1          :S(NEXT)
      DEFINE('PRINT(TABLE,N)I')
*
*   Read a line
*
READ  LINE = INPUT               :F(OUT)
*
*   Count words in separate tables for their lengths
*
AGAIN LINE WORDPAT =             :F(READ)
      GT(SIZE(WORD),8)           :S(AGAIN)
      M = SIZE(WORD)
      ($('LET' M))<WORD> = ($('LET' M))<WORD> + 1      :(AGAIN)
*
*   Print results
*   calling function PRINT for each table
*
OUT   M = 1
PR    PRINT($('LET' M),M)
      M = LT(M,8) M + 1          :S(PR)F(END)
*
*   Code for function PRINT(TABLE,N)
*   prints a table - N is a value used in the headings
*
PRINT
         OUTPUT =
         OUTPUT =
         OUTPUT = 'Table of words with ' N ' letters'
         OUTPUT =
         TABLE = CONVERT(TABLE,'ARRAY')          :F(PRINT.2)
         I = 1
PRINT.1  OUTPUT = TABLE<I,2> ' ' TABLE<I,1>    :F(RETURN)
         I = I + 1                              :(PRINT.1)
*
*   Error message if no words found
*
PRINT.2 OUTPUT = 'No words with ' N ' letters found'
+                                               :(RETURN)
PRINT.END
END
```

In the table name $('LET' M) the brackets are used to ensure that the indirect reference applies to the result of concatenating the string 'LET' and the contents of the variable M. In ($('LET' M))<WORD> note how the brackets are used to ensure that $ operates on the result of concatenating 'LET' and M, not on the contents of the table element subscripted by WORD. In $('LET' M)<WORD>, the contents of that particular table element would be treated as a name.

5. This example shows the use of indirect referencing in gotos.

```
***************************************************************
*
*   Outline program to illustrate indirect referencing in gotos
*
***************************************************************
*
*   Initialisation
*
          &ANCHOR = 1
          &STLIMIT = 10000
          &TRIM = 1
          DEFINE('PROC1()')
          DEFINE('PROC2()')
          DEFINE('PROC3()')
MORE      LINE = INPUT        :F(END)
*
*   Extract the first four characters of LINE and go to
*   the appropriate function
*
          LINE LEN(4) . DATE REM . LINE     :($('D' DATE))
*
D1855     PROC1()             :(MORE)
D1856     PROC2()             :(MORE)
D1857     PROC3()             :(MORE)
*
PROC1
             .
             .
             .
PROC2
             .
             .
             .
PROC3
             .
             .
             .
END
```

The first four characters of each input line are put into DATE. DATE is then concatenated with D and the result is evaluated to give a label to which the program then jumps. The program therefore calls PROC1 if a data line begins with 1855, PROC2 if it begins with 1856 and PROC3 if it begins with 1857.

6. This program makes a new version of its data with the characters $ and & removed from it. The old and new lines are printed out together with the characters which have been removed.

```
***************************************************************
*
*   Program to remove markers from text and print them out
*
***************************************************************
```

```
*
*   Initialisation
*
      &STLIMIT = 10000
      &ANCHOR = 1
      &TRIM = 1
      DEFINE('STRIP(CHARS,TEXT)V1,V2,C')
*
*   Read a line of data and strip markers from it
*
MORE  LINE = INPUT               :F(END)
      OUTPUT = LINE
      REMOVED = STRIP('$&',.LINE)
*
*   Print new version of LINE and markers which have been removed
*
      OUTPUT = LINE
      OUTPUT = 'CHARACTERS REMOVED: ' REMOVED
      OUTPUT =                   :(MORE)
*
*   Function STRIP(CHARS,TEXT) modifies TEXT by removing all
*   instances of CHARS from it and returns
*   those characters which have been removed
*
STRIP $TEXT BREAK(CHARS) . V1 LEN(1) . C REM . V2    :F(RETURN)
      $TEXT = V1 V2
      STRIP = STRIP C            :(STRIP)
STRIP.END
END
```

The name LINE is passed to the function STRIP because LINE is modified by the function. Within the function $TEXT is the argument which is modified.

7   Exercises

7.1   Print out all of the sonnet underlining all occurrences of the letter T.

7.2   Find all the words in the sonnet which contain a doubled letter, i.e. a letter followed by itself.

7.3   Count the number of occurrences of all the words which begin with A, E, I, O and U using a separate table for each vowel.

8 User-Defined Datatypes

In our programs so far we have used a number of different datatypes: arrays, tables, strings, numbers and patterns which are all known to SNOBOL. While these offer some flexibility it is often the case that each item of data has more than one attribute and the representation of the attributes does not easily fit into the SNOBOL datatypes. For example, we may want to record not only how many times each word occurs in a text but also the reference indicating where it occurs. A table such as we have seen up till now can only hold one of these attributes. In order to hold both of them we need to define a new structure or datatype which consists of both a count and a reference, that is an integer and a string. SNOBOL allows the programmer to construct datatypes from any combination of strings, numbers, patterns, arrays and tables. This is a very convenient way of storing attributes and enables a structure to be defined which fits the data, rather than trying to make the data fit SNOBOL's own datatypes.

8.1 Defining Datatypes

The shape of each datatype must first be defined in terms of the components or *fields* from which it is constructed. A name must be given to the datatype and also to each of the fields, using the DATA statement. Its syntax is similar to that of DEFINE.

To define a datatype VOCAB which has the fields COUNT and REFS

        DATA('VOCAB(COUNT,REFS)')

This could, for example, represent a word for which the frequency (COUNT) and references (REFS) are recorded.

There may be several different datatypes in one program. Each must be defined at the beginning with a separate name and field labels.

8.2 Using Datatypes

There will normally be several or many instances of each datatype in a program. We shall call an instance of each datatype an *object*. Each datatype object must be created as one before it can be used.

The following statement creates an object of the VOCAB datatype called A

        A = VOCAB()

for which the fields are initially empty.

Another object of the VOCAB datatype called B would be created as follows

        B = VOCAB()

Once an object has been created as a datatype, its fields can be used. To add 1 to the COUNT field of A

```
COUNT(A) = COUNT(A) + 1
```

To concatenate LNO into the REFS field of A

```
REFS(A) = REFS(A) LNO
```

Information can be put into the object when it is created. If a datatype PERSON has been defined as

```
DATA('PERSON(NAME,AGE,SEX)')
```

the following statement creates an object of the PERSON datatype called FIRSTP and puts TEXT into the NAME field, X into the AGE field and the string 'F' into the field called SEX.

```
FIRSTP = PERSON(TEXT,X,'F')
```

8.3   Datatypes in Arrays and Tables

Each element in a table or array may be a datatype object.

The following lines of program put information into a table called DICT. The element of DICT referenced by DICT<WORD> must first be set up as an object of the VOCAB datatype. The program then adds 1 to its COUNT field and concatenates LINE.NUMBER into its REFS field.

```
     IDENT(DICT<WORD>)                 :F(INCR)
     DICT<WORD> = VOCAB(0)
INCR COUNT(DICT<WORD>) = COUNT(DICT<WORD>) + 1
     REFS(DICT<WORD>) = REFS(DICT<WORD>) LINE.NUMBER
```

Note that each table element has to be created as a VOCAB before it can be used. The statement

```
     IDENT(DICT<WORD>)
```

tests whether a table entry for that word exists (see Section 4.2.2). For new words the statement creates a table entry which contains the null string.

8.4   List Processing

A set of datatype objects may be chained or linked together. This provides a convenient way of storing what otherwise would be a very long string and saving what might be considerable time spent in scanning the string.

Suppose that we were investigating the rhyme scheme of some poetry. We could construct a datatype LIST with three fields. The first two are TEXT for the line of text and NO for the line number. The third field NEXT is itself a LIST which contains the next line of text and its number. It can be thought of as pointing to the next line of text. The datatype can be defined as

```
DATA('LIST(TEXT,NO,NEXT)')
```

Note that the datatype can be defined without specifying the datatypes of its component fields. In this example, NEXT will be identified as a LIST later in the program. We can assume that a version of the poem is accessible which has a letter code denoting the rhyme scheme as the first character on each line. The poem could be

```
AREMEMBER ME WHEN I AM GONE AWAY,
BGONE FAR AWAY INTO THE SILENT LAND;
BWHEN YOU CAN NO MORE HOLD ME BY THE HAND,
ANOR I HALF TURN TO GO YET TURNING STAY.
AREMEMBER ME WHEN NO MORE DAY BY DAY
BYOU TELL ME OF OUR FUTURE THAT YOU PLANNED:
BONLY REMEMBER ME; YOU UNDERSTAND
AIT WILL BE LATE TO COUNSEL THEN OR PRAY.
CYET IF YOU SHOULD FORGET ME FOR A WHILE
DAND AFTERWARDS REMEMBER, DO NOT GRIEVE:
DFOR IF THE DARKNESS AND CORRUPTION LEAVE
EA VESTIGE OF THE THOUGHTS THAT ONCE I HAD,
CBETTER BY FAR YOU SHOULD FORGET AND SMILE
ETHAN THAT YOU SHOULD REMEMBER AND BE SAD.
```

We can make a list of lines which have code A as follows

```
*****************************************************************
*
*   Program to make a list of lines which have code A
*
*****************************************************************
*
*   Initialisation
*
        &ANCHOR = 1
        &TRIM = 1
        &STLIMIT = 10000
        DATA('LIST(TEXT,NO,NEXT)')
*
*   Read a line of data and look for rhyme code A
*
MORE    LINE = INPUT                 :F(OUT)
        LNO = LNO + 1
        LINE 'A' REM . LINE          :F(MORE)
        ACO = ACO + 1
*
*   Record first entry on the list
*
        FIRST = EQ(ACO,1) LIST(LINE,LNO)  :F(ADD)
        L = FIRST                    :(MORE)
*
*   Add subsequent entries
*
ADD     NEXT(L) = LIST(LINE,LNO)
        L = NEXT(L)          :(MORE)
```

LNO is the line number. ACO records the number of occurrences of code A. It also tests whether we are on the first occurrence, using a predicate function combined with an assignment statement (Section 4.2). We must record this separately because it is the head of the list (the first entry) which we need in order to use the list again later in the program, for example to print it out. FIRST is the head of the list. L indicates each LIST on the list in turn. After one line coded A we have

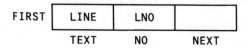

When the second line is found, it is put into the NEXT field of FIRST and can be thought of as pointing to the next entry on the list. This is done by the statement

```
NEXT(L) = LIST(LINE,LNO)
```

This list can then be visualised as

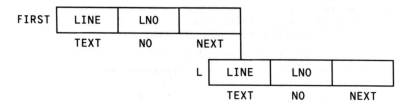

When a new object or entry on the list is made, its NEXT field is empty until the entry following is put on the list. The end of the list is therefore signalled by an object with an empty NEXT field.

The following lines of program could be used to print the list.

```
*
*   Print first entry
*
OUT   L = FIRST
P     OUTPUT = NO(L) ' ' TEXT(L)
*
*   Set L to point to subsequent entries
*
      L = DIFFER(NEXT(L)) NEXT(L)          :S(P)
      OUTPUT =
      OUTPUT = 'Number of rhymes of type A is ' ACO
END
```

Note the use of a predicate function to test for a null string in the NEXT field.

A more sophisticated version of this program could be used to record instances of not just one particular rhyme code but of several. Let us suppose that our data is a sonnet with rhyme scheme ABBAABBACDDECE. The program could begin

```
*****************************************************************
*
*   Program to record instances of several rhyme schemes
*
*****************************************************************
*
*   Initialisation
*
        &ANCHOR = 1
        &TRIM = 1
        &STLIMIT = 10000
        DATA('LIST(TEXT,NO,NEXT)')
        DEFINE('PRINT(HEAD,N)I')
        PAT = LEN(1) . RCODE REM . LINE
*
*   Read a line and look for rhyme code
*
MORE    LINE = INPUT        :F(OUT)
        LNO = LNO + 1
        LINE PAT            :F(MORE)
*
*   RCODES will be a string consisting of all possible codes.
*   Add this code if we have not met it before
*
        RCODES BREAK(RCODE)                     :S(NOTNEW)
        RCODES = RCODES RCODE
NOTNEW  $RCODE = $RCODE + 1
*
*   Head of list
*
        $(RCODE 'F') = EQ($RCODE,1) LIST(LINE,LNO)   :F(ADD)
        $(RCODE 'N') = $(RCODE 'F')                  :(MORE)
*
*   Subsequent entries
*
ADD     NEXT($(RCODE 'N')) = LIST(LINE,LNO)
        $(RCODE 'N') = NEXT($(RCODE 'N'))            :(MORE)
*
```

RCODE is the rhyme scheme for that particular line. $RCODE uses indirect referencing to create a variable to record the count for that rhyme scheme. If RCODE is A,

```
        $RCODE = $RCODE + 1
```

adds 1 to the variable A. If RCODE is B, a variable called B is incremented. Indirect reference is also used to construct names for the head of each list with $(RCODE 'F') and the current position in each list $(RCODE 'N'). If RCODE is A, the head of A is AF and the current position in A is AN.

The lists are printed out as follows

```
OUT     RCODES LEN(1) . RCODE =          :F(END)
        PRINT($(RCODE 'F'),RCODE)        :(OUT)
```

```
*
*   Function PRINT(HEAD,N) prints a list of which the head is HEAD.
*   N is the code for a rhyme scheme
*
PRINT
            I = HEAD
PRINT.1   OUTPUT = NO(I) ' ' TEXT(I)
            I = DIFFER(NEXT(I)) NEXT(I)               :S(PRINT.1)
            OUTPUT =
            OUTPUT = 'Number of rhymes of type ' N ' is ' $N
            OUTPUT =
            OUTPUT =                                  :(RETURN)
PRINT.END
END
```

This program can be written in a more elegant fashion using the name operator . and indirect referencing. A table HEADS is used to store the head of each list. The program begins

```
*****************************************************************
*
*   Program to record instances of several rhyme schemes
*
*****************************************************************
*
*   Initialisation
*
            &ANCHOR = 1
            &TRIM = 1
            &STLIMIT = 10000
            DATA('LIST(TEXT,NO,NEXT)')
            HEADS = TABLE()
            DEFINE('PRINT(HEAD,N)I')
            PAT = LEN(1) . RCODE REM . LINE
*
*   Read a line of data and record rhyme scheme
*
MORE    LINE = INPUT       :F(OUT)
            LNO = LNO + 1
            LINE PAT          :F(MORE)
            RCODES BREAK(RCODE)         :S(ADD)
            RCODES = RCODES RCODE
ADD     $RCODE = $RCODE + 1
*
*   Head of list
*
            HEADS<RCODE> = EQ($RCODE,1) LIST(LINE,LNO)     :S(MORE)
*
*   Subsequent entries on list
*
            ENTRY = .HEADS<RCODE>
TEST    IDENT($ENTRY)                :S(STORE)
            ENTRY = .NEXT($ENTRY)      :(TEST)
STORE   $ENTRY = LIST(LINE,LNO)    :(MORE)
```

The head of each list is stored in HEADS<RCODE> . The statement

```
ENTRY = .HEADS<RCODE>
```

returns the head of the list as a name in ENTRY. $ENTRY then refers to that item. The statements

```
TEST   IDENT($ENTRY)                :S(STORE)
       ENTRY= .NEXT($ENTRY)         :(TEST)
STORE  $ENTRY = LIST(LINE,LNO)      :(MORE)
```

put the next entry on the list and goto MORE. In contrast with the previous program the current position in the list is not retained. Therefore these statements search down the list until an empty NEXT field is found. .NEXT($ENTRY) is the name of the next entry.

The name operator and indirect referencing are used again when the list is printed.

```
OUT    RCODES LEN(1) . RCODE =     :F(END)
       PRINT(HEADS,RCODE)          :(OUT)
*
*  Function PRINT(HEADS,N) prints a list of which HEADS(N)
*  is the head. N is a rhyme code
*
PRINT
       I = .HEADS<N>
PRINT.1 OUTPUT = NO($I) ' ' TEXT($I)
       $I = DIFFER(NEXT($I)) NEXT($I)          :S(PRINT.1)
       OUTPUT =
       OUTPUT = 'Number of rhymes of type ' N ' is '    $N
       OUTPUT =                                :(RETURN)
PRINT.END
END
```

The statement

```
I = .HEADS<N>
```

gives the name of the head of the list. $I can then be used to refer to successive entries in the list.

This program and the previous one both give the same result and well illustrate the point that there is often more than one way of achieving the same objective in SNOBOL. What is most appropriate depends on the data. If in our example there were many instances of each rhyme scheme, it would be better to store the current position in each list. If there were few instances of each of many different rhyme schemes it would be better to search the list to locate the next position.

8   Example Program

This program makes a simple index of the words AND, YOU and ME. The words are
initially stored in a table DICT of objects of datatype VOCAB. Each VOCAB has fields
COUNT to store the count and REFS to store the numbers of the lines where the word
occurs.

```
**********************************************************************
*
*    Program to make an index of the words AND, YOU and ME.
*    The program counts the number of occurrences and prints
*    out the numbers of lines where these words occur
*
**********************************************************************
*
*    Initialisation
*
     &STLIMIT = 10000
     &TRIM = 1
     &ANCHOR = 1
     LETTERS = 'ABCDEFGHIJKLMNOPQRSTUVWXYZ'
     WORDPAT = BREAK(LETTERS) SPAN(LETTERS) . WORD
     DATA('VOCAB(COUNT,REFS)')
     DICT = TABLE()
*
*    Words for index
*
     INDEXWORD = ('AND' | 'YOU' | 'ME') RPOS(0)
*
*    Get words
*    DICT is a table of VOCABs - store COUNT and REFS for
*    each word in the appropriate fields
*
MORE  LINE = INPUT                   :F(OUT)
      LINCO = LINCO + 1
AGAIN LINE WORDPAT =                 :F(MORE)
*
*    Is it a word we want?
*
      WORD INDEXWORD                 :F(AGAIN)
*
*    Creates DICT<WORD> as a VOCAB
*
      IDENT(DICT<WORD>)              :F(YES)
      DICT<WORD> = VOCAB()
*
*    Store count
*
YES   COUNT(DICT<WORD>) = COUNT(DICT<WORD>) + 1
*
*    References are concatenated and separated by commas
*
      REFS(DICT<WORD>) = REFS(DICT<WORD>) LINCO ', '  :(AGAIN)
```

```
*
*  Convert DICT to an array and output in index format
*
OUT    DICT = CONVERT(DICT,'ARRAY')            :F(ERR)
       I = 1
NEXT   OUTPUT = DICT<I,1> '    ' COUNT(DICT<I,2>)        :F(END)
*
*  Delete the last comma and space from REFS
*
       REFS(DICT<I,2>) RTAB(2) . OUTPUT
       OUTPUT =
       I = I + 1                      :(NEXT)
*
*  Error message
*
ERR    OUTPUT = 'Error - program abandoned'
END
```

The output from running this program on the sonnet is shown below.

```
AND    4
10, 11, 13, 14

YOU    7
3, 6, 6, 7, 9, 13, 14

ME    6
1, 3, 5, 6, 7, 9
```

8 Exercises

8.1   Count the number of people employed in each occupation and print out their names and identification numbers under a heading for that occupation.

8.2   Try the list processing technique to store then print out all the lines in the sonnet which end in Y or D.

9 Spitbol

Several different versions of SNOBOL exist, the most common being SPITBOL, which contains some very useful extra features. SPITBOL runs on many different kinds of computers including micros such as the IBM PC. There is in fact more than one version of SPITBOL. The most common one is called Macro SPITBOL, which has been used for the examples in this chapter. SPITBOL is organised within the computer in a different way from SNOBOL with the result that SPITBOL programs run much faster than SNOBOL ones. The features described in this chapter are peculiar to SPITBOL. SNOBOL programs almost always run with SPITBOL. Converting a SPITBOL program to run under SNOBOL may be more difficult.

9.1 Multiple Assignments

In SPITBOL it is possible to write multiple assignment statements.

```
X = Y = 1
```

assigns 1 to both X and Y and is a shorter and neater way of writing

```
X = 1
Y = 1
```

Any number of assignments can be made in one statement.

```
A = B = C = D = E =
```

assigns the null string to A, B, C, D, and E.

9.2 Spitbol Functions

SPITBOL contains a number of additional functions which are not directly accessible in SNOBOL.

9:2.1 BREAKX

BREAKX(string) behaves like BREAK except that it looks ahead beyond the character which has been matched. In

```
LINE = 'LIONS AND LEOPARDS'
LINE BREAK('L') 'LEOPARDS'
```

the pattern fails because the first L is not the L of LEOPARDS and BREAK cannot look any further. In

```
LINE BREAKX('L') 'LEOPARDS'
```

the pattern succeeds because BREAKX recognises that the pattern fails on the first L and looks for another L. It will be seen that BREAKX is actually searching for a string within a string in the anchored mode. Used in this way, it can speed up a program considerably.

BREAKX can also be used to find alternatives.

To find CAT or DOG or MOUSE in LINE and to transfer the one that is found into ANIMAL

```
        LINE BREAKX('CDM') ('CAT' | 'DOG' | 'MOUSE') . ANIMAL
```

BREAKX can be useful when one string is to be replaced by another. The following statements change CAT to DOG in LINE

```
LOOP  LINE BREAKX('C') . V1 'CAT' REM . V2        :F(NEXT)
      LINE = V1 'DOG' V2                          :(LOOP)
NEXT
```

BREAKX is used to split up LINE into three sections; what comes before CAT, which is put into V1, CAT itself, and what comes after CAT, which is put into V2. The new version is then created by concatenating V1, 'DOG' and V2. This is much more efficient than a match and replace statement.

Alternatives can be used in the same way. To change all instances of CAT or DOG or MOUSE into PET

```
LOOP  LINE BREAKX('CDM') . V1 ('CAT' | 'DOG' | 'MOUSE')
+     REM . V2                               :F(NEXT)
      LINE = V1 'PET' V2                     :(LOOP)
NEXT
```

9.2.2 LPAD

LPAD(string1,integer,string2) pads out string1 on the left with string2 until it is integer characters long. String2 must consist of only one character. LPAD is useful for formatting output.

To pad out TEXT on the left with * until it is twelve characters long and assign the result to OUTPUT

```
        OUTPUT = LPAD(TEXT,12,'*')
```

If TEXT contained SNOBOL, this statement would print

```
        ******SNOBOL
```

LPAD is most useful for padding out with spaces, for example to print out items in columns when the items are to be aligned on their endings. If the third argument is omitted, LPAD assumes that it is a space.

If NUMBER had successive values of 3, 129, 36 and 1024

```
        OUTPUT = LPAD(NUMBER,4)
```

would print

```
   3
 129
  36
1024
```

Lists of numbers should always be formatted and LPAD is a very convenient way of doing it. The statement

        OUTPUT = NUMBER

for the same values of number would print

```
3
129
36
1024
```

making the numbers less readable.

9.2.3 RPAD

RPAD(string1,integer,string2) pads out string1 on the right with string2 until it is integer characters long. String2 must consist of only one character. RPAD is useful for formatting output and behaves in exactly the same way as LPAD except that it aligns items to the left of a column.

To pad out TEXT on the right with * until it is twelve characters long and assign the result to OUTPUT

        OUTPUT = RPAD(TEXT,12,'*')

RPAD is most useful if more than one column is to be printed. All columns except the last must be RPADded with spaces so that each following column is aligned.

If ARTIST had successive values of Titian, El Greco, Goya and PAINTING had successive values of Adam and Eve, Adoration of the Shepherds, and The Flower Garden

        OUTPUT = RPAD(ARTIST,15) PAINTING

would print

```
Titian         Adam and Eve
El Greco       Adoration of the Shepherds
Goya           The Flower Garden
```

The statement

        OUTPUT = ARTIST PAINTING

for the same values would print

```
TitianAdam and Eve
El GrecoAdoration of the Shepherds
GoyaThe Flower Garden
```

Inserting a space between the two variables as in

        OUTPUT = ARTIST ' ' PAINTING

would print

```
Titian Adam and Eve
El Greco Adoration of the Shepherds
Goya The Flower Garden
```

The version formatted by RPAD is much more readable.

9.2.4   REVERSE

REVERSE(string) returns the reverse of its string argument.

```
WORD = 'SNOBOL'
OUTPUT = REVERSE(WORD)
```

prints

LOBONS

9.3   Sorting

Sorting items into alphabetical or numerical order is one of the more difficult and time-consuming processes to be performed by the computer. It is often better to use a standard package program for sorting rather than writing a sorting program for a specific purpose.

The Macro SPITBOL implementation of SNOBOL has two built-in functions for sorting. If SPITBOL is not available, and a standard package cannot be used, the programmer must write a user-defined function. Some examples of sorting functions can be found in J. F. Gimpel, *Algorithms in SNOBOL4*, Wiley, 1976, Chapter 13.

9.3.1   SORT

SORT(array,integer) sorts the contents of array into ascending lexical order. It uses the in-built alphabetical order, which differs from one kind of computer to another, and is therefore only suitable for simple sorting. Ascending order means forward alphabetical order for strings. All the computer's characters, including spaces, punctuation and mathematical symbols, have a place in the alphabetical order.

The array must not have more than two dimensions. If it has only one, the elements to be sorted are obvious and the second argument should be omitted. If it has two dimensions, integer gives the number of the column which is to be sorted into order. The first column is used if integer is omitted. For a two-dimensional array, complete rows are re-arranged in accordance with the contents of the column indicated by integer.

SORT returns a sorted array. The following statement sorts the array A.

```
A = SORT(A)
```

The first argument may also be an expression which yields an array.

```
COUNT = SORT(CONVERT(COUNT,'ARRAY'))
```

where COUNT has previously been a table, converts COUNT to an array and sorts the array on the first column.

To sort array A which has two dimensions, on column 3

```
A = SORT(A,3)
```

9.3.2   RSORT

RSORT(array,integer) behaves in the same way as SORT except that the items are rearranged into descending order. For numerical data the order is obvious. For strings, the sorting sequence works backwards through the alphabet so that if all the items to be sorted consisted only of letters, those beginning with Z would be first followed by those beginning with Y, then those beginning with X etc.

To sort array B into descending order

    B = RSORT(B)

To sort array C into descending order on the second column

    C = RSORT(C,2)

9.3.3   Sorting by Endings

If words are to be sorted on their endings, so that words ending in A are first, followed by words ending in B, the words should be loaded into the array backwards. The SPITBOL function REVERSE (Section 9.2.4) is very useful for this. The words should be reversed again for printing.

9.3.4   User-Defined Datatypes and Sorting

An array of objects of a user-defined datatype may be sorted using the SORT or RSORT functions. In this case, the name of the field which is to be used as the key is given as the second argument to the function call. The array must be of one dimension only.

The following statement sorts an array A of objects, of which PLACE and DATE are fields, on the field PLACE. Note that a full stop must be given before the field name to indicate that it is a name. Otherwise the contents of PLACE would be used.

    A = SORT(A,.PLACE)

A second sort key may be given.

To sort the array A described above on the PLACE field, then by DATE

    A = SORT(SORT(A,.DATE),.PLACE)

This has the effect of comparing the DATE field when two elements have the same information in the PLACE field.

9.4   Lexical Predicate Functions

SPITBOL has a full set of lexical predicate functions, that is functions which compare the alphabetical order of strings.

9.4.1   LGE

LGE(string1,string2) succeeds if string1 is lexically greater than or equal to string2. The alphabetical order used is the same as that for LGT and for sorting. Upper and lower case letters are not treated as being equal.

```
LGE(TEXT1,TEXT2)
```

succeeds if TEXT1 is the same as TEXT2 or comes after it in alphabetical order.

9.4.2   LLE

LLE(string1,string2) succeeds if string1 is lexically less than or equal to string2.

```
LLE(TEXT1,TEXT2)
```

succeeds if TEXT1 is the same as TEXT2 or comes before it in alphabetical order.

9.4.3   LLT

LLT(string1,string2) succeeds if string1 is lexically less than string2.

```
LLE(TEXT1,TEXT2)
```

succeeds if TEXT1 comes before TEXT2 in alphabetical order.

9.4.4   LEQ

LEQ(string1,string2) tests whether string1 and string2 are lexically equal. In contrast with IDENT, the arguments are converted to strings.

```
X = 23
Y = '23'
LEQ(X,Y)
```

succeeds because X is converted to the string 23.

```
IDENT(X,Y)
```

fails because X is a number and Y is a string.

9.4.5   LNE

LNE(string1,string2) succeeds if string1 and string2 are lexically not equal. In contrast with DIFFER, the arguments are converted to strings.

```
X = 23
Y = '23'
LNE(X,Y)
```

fails because X is converted to the string 23.

9   Example Programs

1.   This program counts the occurrences of words which contain LY or LEY.

```
****************************************************************
*
*    Program to count the number of words which contain LY
*    or LEY
*
****************************************************************
*
*    Initialisation
*
      &STLIMIT = 10000
      &TRIM = 1
      &ANCHOR = 1
      LETTERS = 'ABCDEFGHIJKLMNOPQRSTUVWXYZ'
      WORDPAT = BREAK(LETTERS) SPAN(LETTERS) . WORD
      LYWORDS = BREAKX('L') ('LY' | 'LEY')
*
*   Read data and count words
*
MORE  LINE = INPUT              :F(PRINT)
AGAIN LINE WORDPAT =            :F(MORE)
      WORD LYWORDS              :F(AGAIN)
      COUNT = COUNT + 1         :(AGAIN)
*
*   Print results
*
PRINT OUTPUT = DUPL(' ',10) 'There are ' COUNT
+ ' words containing "LY" or "LEY"'
END
```

BREAKX is used in the pattern LYWORDS to find LY or LEY.

2.   Abbreviations which are not in fixed positions may be found using BREAKX. This program makes a new version of its data with PROF$ expanded to Professor, REV$ expanded to Reverend, LN$ to London and NY$ to New York

```
****************************************************************
*
*    Program to make a new version of data with
*    abbreviations expanded
*
****************************************************************
*
*    Initialisation
*
      &ANCHOR = 1
      &STLIMIT = 10000
      &TRIM = 1
      ABBREV = TABLE(4)
      ABBREV<'PROF$'> = 'Professor'
      ABBREV<'REV$'> = 'Reverend'
      ABBREV<'LN$'> = 'London'
      ABBREV<'NY$'> = 'New York'
```

```
       PAT = BREAKX('PRLN') . PARTONE
+ ('PROF$' | 'REV$' | 'LN$' | 'NY$') . TEXT REM . PARTTWO
*
*  Read a line
*
MORE  LINE = INPUT        :F(END)
*
*  Test for abbreviations.
*  There may be more than one in each line
*
AGAIN LINE PAT            :F(PRINT)
*
*  If found, expand abbreviation
*
       LINE = PARTONE ABBREV<TEXT> PARTTWO :(AGAIN)
*
*  Print line
*
PRINT OUTPUT = LINE       :(MORE)
END
```

Using BREAKX in this way is much more efficient than using match and replace statements to test for all the abbreviations. If the input line was

```
PROF$ Smith is in LN$, but REV$ Jones is in NY$.
```

the line would be transformed as follows

```
Professor Smith is in LN$, but REV$ Jones is in NY$.
Professor Smith is in London, but REV$ Jones is in NY$.
Professor Smith is in London, but Reverend Jones is in NY$.
Professor Smith is in London, but Reverend Jones is in New York.
```

before being output.

3. This program makes a word count of all words. The words are given in forward alphabetical order, in descending frequency order and in alphabetical order of their endings.

```
****************************************************************
*
*  Program to make a word count of all words. The words are
*  given in forward alphabetical order, descending
*  frequency order and in alphabetical order of their
*  endings
*
****************************************************************
*
*  Initialisation
*
       &STLIMIT = 10000
       &ANCHOR = &TRIM = 1
       LETTERS = 'ABCDEFGHIJKLMNOPQRSTUVWXYZ'
       WORDPAT = BREAK(LETTERS) SPAN(LETTERS) . WORD
       COUNT = TABLE()
       DEFINE('REVARRAY(B)I')
       DEFINE('PRINT(WORDS,TYPE)I,J,L,TEXT')
```

```
*
*   Read a line and count words in table COUNT
*
READ  LINE = INPUT                              :F(OUT)
NEXT  LINE WORDPAT =                            :F(READ)
      COUNT<WORD> = COUNT<WORD> + 1             :(NEXT)
*
*   Print results after sorting array.
*   Array must be reversed for sort on endings
*   and reversed again for printing
*
OUT   COUNT = CONVERT(COUNT,'ARRAY')       :F(ERR)
      A = SORT(COUNT)
      PRINT(A,'Forward Sort')
      A = RSORT(COUNT,2)
      PRINT(A,'Descending Sort')
      A = SORT(REVARRAY(COUNT))
      A = REVARRAY(A)
      PRINT(A,'Reverse Sort')                   :(END)
*
*   Code for function PRINT which prints array WORDS with
*   heading TYPE
*
PRINT
          OUTPUT =
*
*   Print heading in centre of 80 character wide page and
*   underline heading with - signs
*
          L = (80 - SIZE(TYPE)) / 2
          OUTPUT = DUPL(' ',L) TYPE
          OUTPUT = DUPL(' ',L) DUPL('-',SIZE(TYPE))
          OUTPUT =
          I = 1
*
*   Words and their frequencies are printed in columns
*   across the page
*
PRINT.1   J = 1
PRINT.2   TEXT = TEXT LPAD(WORDS<I,2>,4) ' ' RPAD(WORDS<I,1>,15)
+                                        :F(PRINT.3)
          I = I + 1
          J = LT(J,4) J + 1               :S(PRINT.2)
          OUTPUT = TEXT
          TEXT =                          :(PRINT.1)
*
*   Print last (incomplete) line if there is one
*
PRINT.3   EQ(REMDR(I - 1,4),0)            :S(RETURN)
          OUTPUT = TEXT                   :(RETURN)
PRINT.END
```

```
*
*   Function REVARRAY(B) reverses each element
*   of the first column of array B
*
REVARRAY
            I = 1
REVARRAY.1 B<I,1> = REVERSE(B<I,1>)        :F(REVARRAY.2)
            I = I + 1                      :(REVARRAY.1)
REVARRAY.2 REVARRAY = B                    :(RETURN)
REVARRAY.END
*
*   Error message if table is empty
*
ERR     OUTPUT = 'No words found'
END
```

When the end of the data is reached the table COUNT is converted into an array called COUNT. The array is first sorted on the first column by SORT and then printed under a heading Forward Sort. RSORT is used on the second column to sort the words by frequency with the most frequent word first. All the elements in the first column of A are reversed before SORT is called again to sort the words on their endings. They are reversed again before being printed under a heading Reverse Sort.

LPAD and RPAD are used in the function PRINT to print the words together with their frequencies in four columns across the page. I is the subscript which indicates the row of the array. The words and their frequencies are concatenated into TEXT using LPAD and RPAD to line them up in columns. J counts the words as they are put into TEXT and TEXT is printed when J reaches 4. TEXT is then emptied and J set to 1 before the next four words are dealt with. When the end of the array is reached, there will be an incomplete line left in TEXT unless the number of rows in the array is exactly divisible by 4. The statement

```
PRINT.3  EQ(REMDR(I - 1,4),0)        :S(RETURN)
```

determines whether there is an incomplete line to be printed. If so, it is printed by

```
        OUTPUT = TEXT                :(RETURN)
```

4.   This program counts the number of paintings by each artist and prints them out in alphabetical order of the artists' names.

The data is

```
TPThe Immaculate Conception
RAThe Madonna of the Fish
TISt Margaret and the Dragon
RAPortrait of a Cardinal
EGThe Holy Trinity
VLThe Forge of Vulcan
VLLas Meninas
GYThe Family of Charles IV
TIVenus and Adonis
VLThe Infanta Margarita
TIThe Entombment
GYThe Third of May 1808
```

```
******************************************************************
*
*   Program to count the number of paintings by each artist
*
******************************************************************
*
*   Initialisation
*
        &STLIMIT = 10000
        &ANCHOR = 1
        &TRIM = 1
        COUNT = TABLE()
*
        ARTISTS = TABLE(6)
        ARTISTS<'RA'> = 'Raphael'
        ARTISTS<'TI'> = 'Titian'
        ARTISTS<'TP'> = 'Tiepolo'
        ARTISTS<'EG'> = 'El Greco'
        ARTISTS<'VL'> = 'Velazquez'
        ARTISTS<'GY'> = 'Goya'
*
        FINDARTIST = LEN(2) . ARTIST REM . TITLE
*
*   Read a line and count artists
*
MORE  LINE = INPUT       :F(PRINT)
        LINE FINDARTIST
        COUNT<ARTISTS<ARTIST>> = COUNT<ARTISTS<ARTIST>> + 1   :(MORE)
*
*   Print totals
*
PRINT
        COUNT = SORT(CONVERT(COUNT,'ARRAY'))                  :F(EMPTY)
        OUTPUT = 'Count of artists'
        OUTPUT =
        I = 1
AGAIN OUTPUT = LPAD(COUNT<I,2>,4) ' ' COUNT<I,1>      :F(END)
        I = I + 1            :(AGAIN)
EMPTY OUTPUT = 'No artists found'
END
```

The output is

```
Count of artists

    1  El Greco
    2  Goya
    2  Raphael
    1  Tiepolo
    3  Titian
    3  Velazquez
```

Note that the numbers are printed before the artists' names. They are less easy to read when printed after them. If the output statement was

```
AGAIN OUTPUT = RPAD(COUNT<I,1>,15) LPAD(COUNT<I,2>,4)        :F(END)
```

the output would be

```
Count of artists

El Greco         1
Goya             2
Raphael          2
Tiepolo          1
Titian           3
Velazquez        3
```

The statement

```
        COUNT<ARTISTS<ARTIST>> = COUNT<ARTISTS<ARTIST>> + 1    :(MORE)
```

ensures that the full version of the artist's name, not the code, is used as the table subscript. ARTIST is the code for the artist. ARTISTS<ARTIST> is the full name of the artist. The codes must be translated to the full names of the artists before the names are sorted. If the sort is done on the codes, it may not yield the correct alphabetical order for the full names.

5.   If we add a date to each painting so that the data becomes

```
TP1767The Immaculate Conception
RA1514The Madonna of the Fish
TI1565St Margaret and the Dragon
RA1509Portrait of a Cardinal
EG1577The Holy Trinity
VL1630The Forge of Vulcan
VL1656Las Meninas
GY1808The Family of Charles IV
TI1553Venus and Adonis
VL1660The Infanta Margarita
TI1559The Entombment
GY1808The Third of May 1808
```

we can use a program which sorts datatypes to sort the paintings by artist and by date. If two paintings have the same artist they are put into chronological order

```
******************************************************************
*
*   Program to sort the paintings by artist and by date
*
******************************************************************
*
*   Initialisation
*
        &STLIMIT = 10000
        &ANCHOR = 1
```

```
      &TRIM = 1
      ARTISTS = TABLE(6)
      ARTISTS<'RA'> = 'Raphael'
      ARTISTS<'TI'> = 'Titian'
      ARTISTS<'TP'> = 'Tiepolo'
      ARTISTS<'EG'> = 'El Greco'
      ARTISTS<'VL'> = 'Velazquez'
      ARTISTS<'GY'> = 'Goya'
*
      N = 12
      PAINTINGS = ARRAY(N)
      DATA('PAINTING(NAME,YEAR,TITLE)')
*
      PAT = LEN(2) . ARTIST LEN(4) . DATE REM . TITLE
*
*  Read a line
*
      I = 1
MORE  LINE = INPUT       :F(SORTS)
*
*  Extract fields and load them into PAINTINGS.
*  Each element of PAINTINGS is a PAINTING
*
      LINE PAT
      PAINTINGS<I> = PAINTING(ARTISTS<ARTIST>,DATE,TITLE)
      I = I + 1                  :(MORE)
*
*  Sort array of datatypes on NAME then YEAR
*
SORTS PAINTINGS = SORT(SORT(PAINTINGS,.YEAR),.NAME)
*
*  Print array
*
      I = 1
      NEWNAME = NAME(PAINTINGS<I>)
*
*  Only print name if it is different from previous one
*
NEW   OUTPUT =
      OUTPUT = NEWNAME
SAME  OUTPUT = DUPL(' ',5) RPAD(YEAR(PAINTINGS<I>),6)
+  TITLE(PAINTINGS<I>)
      I = LT(I,N) I + 1                          :F(END)
*
*  Check for same artist
*
      IDENT(NAME(PAINTINGS<I>),NEWNAME)         :S(SAME)
      NEWNAME = NAME(PAINTINGS<I>)              :(NEW)

END
```

The results are printed out in catalogue format as shown below.

```
El Greco
     1577  The Holy Trinity

Goya
     1808  The Family of Charles IV
     1808  The Third of May 1808

Raphael
     1509  Portrait of a Cardinal
     1514  The Madonna of the Fish

Tiepolo
     1767  The Immaculate Conception

Titian
     1553  Venus and Adonis
     1559  The Entombment
     1565  St Margaret and the Dragon

Velazquez
     1630  The Forge of Vulcan
     1656  Las Meninas
     1660  The Infanta Margarita
```

The name of the artist is only printed if it is different from the previous one. The name of the first artist is put into NEWNAME by

```
     I = 1
     NEWNAME = NAME(PAINTINGS<I>)
```

After the name is printed by

```
     OUTPUT = NEWNAME
```

the date and title of the painting are printed by

```
SAME   OUTPUT = DUPL(' ',5) RPAD(YEAR(PAINTINGS<I>,6)
+    TITLE(PAINTINGS<I>)
```

I is incremented by 1 to get the next painting. The statement

```
     IDENT(NAME(PAINTINGS<I>),NEWNAME)        :S(SAME)
```

tests whether its NAME field is the same as NEWNAME (the one we have just printed). If it is, the program goes to SAME and prints only the date and title of that painting. If the name is not the same, NEWNAME becomes the NAME field of the new painting and the program goes to NEW to print a blank line and the name.

9   Exercises

These exercises are for SPITBOL, or they can be done using user-defined functions for SORT, LPAD, RPAD and BREAKX taken from Gimpel.

9.1   Make a word list of all the words in the sonnet and print out the words in alphabetical order together with their frequencies. Line them up in four columns.

9.2   Make a catalogue of all the people ordered by place of birth then by date of birth.

9.3   Print out all of the sonnet with REMEMBER changed to FORGET, using the anchored mode.

10 Diagnosing Errors

Programs rarely work the first time. SNOBOL provides various ways of assisting the detection of errors in a program. These error detection features vary in different versions of SNOBOL and SPITBOL. The technical documentation which accompanies each version should be consulted for exact details.

10.1 Dumping

A dump gives a list of all the variables in a program and their contents.

10.1.1 &DUMP

The keyword &DUMP can be set to a value of 1 or 2 at the beginning of a program. When it is set to 1, the value of all non-null variables is printed out when the program terminates. A value of 2 causes all non-null array, table and user-defined datatypes to be printed as well. The format of the dump varies depending on the implementation of SNOBOL. A typical dump from Macro SPITBOL is given below. It will be seen that the word PATTERN is printed as the value of a variable which contains a pattern, not the pattern itself.

The program data is

```
REMEMBER ME WHEN I AM GONE AWAY,
GONE FAR AWAY INTO THE SILENT LAND;
WHEN YOU CAN NO MORE HOLD ME BY THE HAND,
NOR I HALF TURN TO GO YET TURNING STAY.
```

```
**********************************************************************
*
*   Program to count the number of words which begin with a vowel
*
**********************************************************************
*
*   Initialisation
*
        &STLIMIT = 10000
        &ANCHOR = 1
        &TRIM = 1
        &DUMP = 1
        LETTERS = 'ABCDEFGHIJKLMNOPQRSTUVWXYZ'
        WORDPAT = BREAK(LETTERS) SPAN(LETTERS) . WORD
        VOWELPAT = ANY('AEIOU')
        COUNT = TABLE()
```

```
*
*  Read a line and count words beginning with a vowel
*
READ  LINE = INPUT       :F(PRINT)
NEXT  LINE WORDPAT =      :F(READ)
      WORD VOWELPAT       :F(NEXT)
      COUNT<WORD> = COUNT<WORD> + 1          :(NEXT)
*
*  Print results
*
PRINT HEAD = 'Count of words beginning with a vowel'
      OUTPUT = HEAD
      OUTPUT = DUPL('-',SIZE(HEAD))
      OUTPUT =
      COUNT = CONVERT(COUNT,'ARRAY')          :F(EMPTY)
      I = 1
AGAIN OUTPUT = COUNT<I,2> ' ' COUNT<I,1>   :F(END)
      I = I + 1        :(AGAIN)
EMPTY OUTPUT = 'No words found'
END


Count of words beginning with a vowel
-------------------------------------

1  INTO
2  AWAY
2  I
1  AM


DUMP OF NATURAL VARIABLES

COUNT = ARRAY(4,2) £2
HEAD = 'Count of words beginning with a vowel'
I = 5
INPUT = 'NOR I HALF TURN TO GO YET TURNING STAY.'
LETTERS = 'ABCDEFGHIJKLMNOPQRSTUVWXYZ'
LINE = '.'
OUTPUT = '1   AM'
VOWELPAT = PATTERN
WORD = 'STAY'
WORDPAT = PATTERN
```

The dump prints the contents of all variables at the end of execution unless the value is
null. Although they are not shown here, the dump also prints the values of all the
SNOBOL keywords which the programmer is allowed to alter, whether these have been
assigned by the program or are defaults. The keywords are different in SNOBOL and
SPITBOL, but some are common to both. Full details about them may be found in the
technical documentation for a particular implementation of SNOBOL.

10.1.2   DUMP Function

The keyword &DUMP causes the dump to be produced at the end of the execution of the program. The execution ends either by reaching the label END, a normal end, or by an execution error, an abnormal end. A dump at the end may not necessarily show up an error which occurs earlier in the program.

A call to the function DUMP can be used to cause a dump anywhere in a program. DUMP has one argument which is an integer number. A value of 1 or 2 causes the same kinds of dump as the keyword &DUMP. If the argument is null or zero, no dump is produced. The argument can thus be used to turn the dump on and off when required.

```
*****************************************************************
*
*    Program to count words which begin with a vowel
*
*****************************************************************
*
*    Initialisation
*
      &STLIMIT = 10000
      &ANCHOR = 1
      &TRIM = 1
      LETTERS = 'ABCDEFGHIJKLMNOPQRSTUVWXYZ'
      WORDPAT = BREAK(LETTERS) SPAN(LETTERS) . WORD
      VOWELPAT = ANY('AEIOU')
      COUNT = TABLE()
*
*    Read a line and count words beginning with a vowel
*
READ  LINE = INPUT        :F(PRINT)
      LNO = LNO + 1
*
*    Dump on for odd-numbered lines
*
      X = REMDR(LNO,2)
      DUMP(X)
NEXT  LINE WORDPAT =       :F(READ)
      WORD VOWELPAT        :F(NEXT)
      COUNT<WORD> = COUNT<WORD> + 1      :(NEXT)
*
*    Print results
*
PRINT HEAD = 'Count of words beginning with a vowel'
      OUTPUT = HEAD
      OUTPUT = DUPL('-',SIZE(HEAD))
      OUTPUT =
      COUNT = CONVERT(COUNT,'ARRAY')             :F(EMPTY)
      I = 1
AGAIN OUTPUT = COUNT<I,2> '  ' COUNT<I,1>    :F(END)
      I = I + 1         :(AGAIN)
EMPTY OUTPUT = 'No words found'
END
```

```
DUMP OF NATURAL VARIABLES

COUNT = TABLE(11) £1
INPUT = 'REMEMBER ME WHEN I AM GONE AWAY,'
LETTERS = 'ABCDEFGHIJKLMNOPQRSTUVWXYZ'
LINE = 'REMEMBER ME WHEN I AM GONE AWAY,'
LNO = 1
VOWELPAT = PATTERN
WORDPAT = PATTERN
X = 1

DUMP OF NATURAL VARIABLES

COUNT = TABLE(11) £1
INPUT = 'WHEN YOU CAN NO MORE HOLD ME BY THE HAND,'
LETTERS = 'ABCDEFGHIJKLMNOPQRSTUVWXYZ'
LINE = 'WHEN YOU CAN NO MORE HOLD ME BY THE HAND,'
LNO = 3
VOWELPAT = PATTERN
WORD = 'LAND'
WORDPAT = PATTERN
X = 1

Count of words beginning with a vowel
-------------------------------------

1   INTO
2   AWAY
2   I
1   AM
```

The dump of keywords has been omitted.

10.2 TRACE

The trace facilities allow the use of one or more variables or other names to be recorded throughout the execution of a program. Both the keyword &TRACE and the function TRACE are required to set up a trace. The following actions can be traced

VALUE	change in the value of a variable
CALL	call to a function
RETURN	return from a function
FUNCTION	function call and return
KEYWORD	change in the value of a keyword
LABEL	branch to a label

SPITBOL has an extra action:

ACCESS	access to a variable

The function TRACE gives the name to be traced and the type of action to be traced.

```
TRACE(.WORD,'VALUE')
```

requests a trace of each new value of the variable WORD.

```
TRACE(.NEXT,'LABEL')
```

requests a trace of each goto which branches to the label NEXT.

```
TRACE(.PRINT,'FUNCTION')
```

requests a trace of each call to and return from the function PRINT.

The keyword &TRACE must have a positive value for the tracing to be carried out. Its value is decremented by 1 for each line of tracing which is printed. When its value reaches zero, no more tracing is printed.

To print the first 50 changes in the value of WORD, both the following statements are required.

```
&TRACE = 50
TRACE(.WORD,'VALUE')
```

The use of &TRACE means that tracing can be turned on and off without the need to remove calls to the TRACE function from the program. The keyword &FTRACE can be used to trace a call to and return from each function. &FTRACE must be set to a positive value at the beginning of a program and again its value is decremented by 1 for each trace line that is printed until it reaches 0.

A simple program with tracing is shown below. The format of the tracing is that produced by Macro SPITBOL.

```
*****************************************************************
*
*   Program to count the total number of words in the data
*
*****************************************************************
*
*   Initialisation
*
        &STLIMIT = 10000
        &ANCHOR = 1
        &TRIM = 1
*
        &TRACE = 10
        TRACE(.LINE,'VALUE')
*
        LETTERS = 'ABCDEFGHIJKLMNOPQRSTUVWXYZ'
        WORDPAT = BREAK(LETTERS) SPAN(LETTERS)
*
*   Read a line and count words
*
MORE    LINE = INPUT       :F(PRINT)
NEXT    LINE WORDPAT =      :F(MORE)
        COUNT = COUNT + 1 :(NEXT)
*
*   Print results
*
PRINT OUTPUT = 'The number of words is ' COUNT
END
```

```
****8******* LINE = 'REMEMBER ME WHEN I AM GONE AWAY,'
****9******* LINE = ' ME WHEN I AM GONE AWAY,'
****9******* LINE = ' WHEN I AM GONE AWAY,'
****9******* LINE = ' I AM GONE AWAY,'
****9******* LINE = ' AM GONE AWAY,'
****9******* LINE = ' GONE AWAY,'
****9******* LINE = ' AWAY,'
****9******* LINE = ','
****8******* LINE = 'GONE FAR AWAY INTO THE SILENT LAND;'
****9******* LINE = ' FAR AWAY INTO THE SILENT LAND;'
The number of words is 14
```

Tracing is turned on for the first ten changes to the value of LINE. The number within the asterisks is the number of the statement, not counting comment lines, where the change in the value of LINE occurs.

10.3   &ERRLIMIT

Two types of error conditions are recognised. Conditionally fatal errors are those from which it is possible to recover and continue execution of the program. Unconditionally fatal errors cause the program to stop whatever happens. The keyword &ERRLIMIT can be used to specify how many conditionally fatal errors are allowed before the program stops. For example

&ERRLIMIT = 15

allows 15 conditionally fatal errors to occur before the program terminates. Each such error is treated as a statement failure. &ERRLIMIT behaves like &TRACE in that its value is decremented by 1 for each error until it becomes 0.

Note that the use of &ERRLIMIT is different in SPITBOL. (See the next section.)

10.3.1   SETEXIT and &ERRLIMIT

A more sophisticated way of using &ERRLIMIT exists in SPITBOL. This requires the function SETEXIT which is used to intercept execution errors. SETEXIT has one argument, which is the name of a label. If an execution error occurs, the program jumps to that label if &ERRLIMIT has a value greater than zero. &ERRLIMIT is therefore used to control the number of interceptions that can be made. The label normally introduces an error routine, a section of program which decides what to do after an error condition. The error routine can make use of

&ERRTYPE   the error number (as allocated by the version of SPITBOL)
&ERRTEXT   the text of the error message
&LASTNO   the number of the last statement executed

From these it can determine whether the program is able to carry on or not.

The error routine can also make use of special labels in a goto.

ABORT   terminates execution. The error is handled as if it had not been intercepted.

CONTINUE   The program returns to the statement which caused the error and
                    from there immediately to the failure exit of this statement.
any label   The program goes to another label elsewhere in the program.
RETURN   If the error has occurred within a function, the program im-
                    mediately returns from the function.

When one error has been intercepted, the effect of SETEXIT is cancelled. Therefore if
the interception of further errors is required, the error routine must call SETEXIT
again.

The following program uses SETEXIT to intercept errors in the data, which consists of
a date followed by the title of a painting.

```
1767The Immaculate Conception
1514The Madonna of the Fish
15e5St Margaret and the Dragon
1509Portrait of a Cardinal
1577The Holy Trinity
1630The Forge of Vulcan
166tLas Meninas
1808The Family of Charles IV
1553Venus and Adonis
1660The Infanta Margarita
1559The Entombment
1808The Third of May 1808
```

Deliberate errors have been inserted into the dates 15e5 and 166t.

```
********************************************************************
*
*   Program to print out paintings with date after 1550.
*   SETEXIT is used to intercept errors in the data
*
********************************************************************
*
*   Initialisation
*
      &STLIMIT = 10000
      &ANCHOR = 1
      &TRIM = 1
      SETEXIT(.DATAERROR)
      &ERRLIMIT = 20
*
*   Deliberate error
*
      X = 'ABC'
*
*   Read data and print out required lines
*
MORE  LINE = INPUT                    :F(END)
      LINE LEN(4) . DATE REM . TEXT
      GT(DATE,1550)                   :F(MORE)
      OUTPUT = DATE ' ' TEXT
      TEXT 'Venus'                    :F(MORE)
      OUTPUT = DUPL(' ',X) TEXT       :(MORE)
```

```
*
*  Error routine to intercept incorrect data
*
DATAERROR
     EQ(&ERRTYPE,111)                 :F(TRUEERROR)
     OUTPUT =
     OUTPUT = '*** ' LINE
     OUTPUT = '*** First four characters are not a number'
     OUTPUT =
     SETEXIT(.DATAERROR)              :(CONTINUE)
*
*  Error routine for other errors
*
TRUEERROR
     OUTPUT =
     OUTPUT = '*** Error ' &ERRTYPE ' at statement ' &LASTNO
     OUTPUT = '*** ' &ERRTEXT
END
```

SPITBOL error number 111 which indicates that the first argument to GT is not numeric is intercepted and an error message is printed by the statements

```
     OUTPUT =
     OUTPUT = '*** ' LINE
     OUTPUT = '*** First four characters are not a number'
```

The program is then allowed to continue. The statement

```
     EQ(&ERRTYPE,111)         :F(TRUEERROR)
```

ensures that only error 111 is dealt with in this way. If &ERRTYPE is another number, the program goes to TRUEERROR and prints an error message before terminating.

The variable X has been deliberately set to ABC to cause an error with DUPL in the statement

```
     OUTPUT = DUPL(' ',X) TEXT    :(MORE)
```

to show what happens if another error occurs. The output is

```
1767  The Immaculate Conception

*** 15e5St Margaret and the Dragon
*** First four characters are not a number

1577  The Holy Trinity
1630  The Forge of Vulcan

*** 166tLas Meninas
*** First four characters are not a number

1808  The Family of Charles IV
1553  Venus and Adonis

*** Error 90 at statement 21

*** DUPL SECOND ARGUMENT IS NOT INTEGER
```

11   Using SNOBOL

11.1   Some Applications for Snobol

SNOBOL is suitable for many applications in the humanities. Here only a brief description of some of the more common ones is given.

11.1.1   Word Counts and Concordances

Word counts and concordances are the most obvious applications of computers to literature and programs to generate them are easier to write in SNOBOL than in any other computer language. We have already seen word count programs in Chapter 5 Example 1 and Chapter 9 Example 3 and an index of selected words in the example program in Chapter 8. More sophisticated concordances can of course be made by a standard program such as the Oxford Concordance Program (OCP), if one is available.

11.1.2   Preparing Text for Concordances

SNOBOL can be very useful as an aid to preparing text for computer analysis. The researcher may have acquired a computer-readable version of his text and may wish to reformat it or to alter a coding scheme. For very simple alterations a computer's own editor may be sufficient, but a SNOBOL program is usually the best way of making all the required alterations in one pass of the text. The concordance user could use SNOBOL to ensure that text references such as title, chapter, and page are in a suitable form for OCP. If the text has been entered by an optical character reader such as the Kurzweil Data Entry Machine, a program can pick up page boundaries or headers and reformat them into text references.

Example 2 in Chapter 9 shows how names or other often occurring items can be input in an abbreviated form and expanded to the correct form using a table. This not only saves typing time but also ensures that the names are always spelled correctly. If SPITBOL is not available, a version of this program can be written using a match and replace statement instead of BREAKX.

11.1.3   Bibliographies

Bibliographies are another obvious computer application in the humanities. Each book or article is a record which is divided into a number of fields for, say, author, title and publisher, in other words a SNOBOL datatype. SNOBOL is the best language for writing a bibliography program because it handles variable length strings so easily, but an alternative is to use a standard program. FAMULUS is perhaps the best-known bibliography package. Data for FAMULUS has to be in a specific form with field labels at the beginning of each field or category such as author, title and publisher. A program can be written to reformat data which has been input in a more compact form into a form suitable for FAMULUS.

11.1.4   Typesetting and Text Formatting

Text formatting programs use codes to indicate the end of a paragraph and for headings, titles, running headers and footers. Computer programs for typesetting also need extra information embedded in the text, for example to change typeface or to use italic or bold and also to access characters which are not on the normal computer keyboard. Some of these codes can be cumbersome to input at each point in the text. A better method is sometimes to input them in a simple form then use a program to expand them to the instructions for the relevant typesetter or text formatter.

The text of this book was first input to a computer with instructions for a text formatter. For typesetting on the Lasercomp at Oxford University Computing Service, a SNOBOL program was written which converted the text formatting commands to those for the Lasercomp and picked up from the text extra features needed for the typesetter. These included program variables to be set in OCR-B in the middle of a line of text in Times New Roman, and the word SNOBOL to be in small capitals and letter-spaced. Although the program could not find every case (in particular it could not distinguish between the variable A and the word A), it was much easier to write the program to do most of the work and to correct the rest by hand.

SNOBOL can easily be used to insert typesetting commands for a concordance or bibliography. In a bibliography, for example, the title field could be italic, the author's name perhaps standardised in one form, e.g. initials then surname, and each entry set with commas between the sections. In a concordance the headword could be picked out in bold and the entries lined up on the keywords.

11.1.5   Data Validation and Preparation

Exercise 6.2 is a simple use of SNOBOL for validating data. This could be expanded to many more fields, for example to check that the dates are within possible ranges. A program could also generate extra fields. A simple example is the conversion of dates from the form of day month year, e.g. 10 March 1923 into a numerical form suitable for sorting e.g. 19230310. A more sophisticated example could be the treatment of dates which span both BC and AD. Dates such as 29BC and AD29 cannot be sorted into the correct chronological order as they stand. One solution is to generate an extra field from these dates which consists of a code which is used for sorting the dates.

11.1.6   Metrical Analysis

Computers can analyse the metre of verse which is scanned either by length of syllable or by stress. In either case a special purpose program is needed. SNOBOL is an ideal language for this as patterns defining the different values for a syllable can be built up. Conversion of a text into a phonetic or metrical form is usually done by looking up each word in a dictionary where the corresponding metrical form has been stored. The table facility in SNOBOL is an obvious and easy way of handling the dictionary.

11.1.7   Drawing Diagrams

Results printed in the form of a bar chart or diagram are easier for the reader to interpret than tables of numbers or words. On the screen or printer, diagrams can be drawn using vertical bars for vertical lines and minus signs for horizontal lines. A bar chart could be drawn by a row of asterisks and the simplest way of doing this is the function DUPL. DUPL('*',X) prints X asterisks. DUPL can also be used to print spaces between various sections of a diagram. The cursor position operator ﹫ is a useful way of recording the position of an item so that a marker can be printed underneath it.

11.1.8   Syntax Analysers and Parsers

Although parsing of literary texts is not feasible without considerable human intervention, SNOBOL is an excellent language to experiment with parsing procedures, using the pattern facilities to build up definitions. SNOBOL tables are a very easy way of organising any kind of dictionary look-up, although they can become slow in execution if the table is large.

11.2   Snobol on Different Computers

SNOBOL can be run on many different computers, both large mainframes and small microcomputers.

11.2.1   Mainframe Computers

Implementations of SNOBOL exist for major mainframe computers. All are priced for the academic market and are therefore relatively cheap for a university computer centre to buy. For some computer ranges there is a choice of several implementations.

SNOBOL is strictly speaking what is called an *interpreter*, that is the computer interprets the program as it is input. This is in contrast with a *compiler* such as SPITBOL, where the computer deals with the program in two stages. The first is known as compilation where the computer translates the program into its own low level language and marks any errors which it has found. When this translation process is complete, the program is then executed. Compilers are generally faster to run than interpreters.

The version of SNOBOL which is generally considered to be the best is a compiler called Macro SPITBOL which has been implemented on several machine ranges.

11.2.2   Implementation Specific Features

Each implementation has some features which are specific to that implementation. Different implementations have different initial values for the SNOBOL keywords and in some cases different keywords. Each version also has *compiler directives* which determine such features as the maximum length of a line in a SNOBOL program, or whether the program is to be listed on the printer or merely its results. It is possible to reset the compiler directives and the implementation manual should be consulted for this.

Within one program input can be taken from more than one set of data or file. This means that sets of data can be merged together or that a program can read the data from one file and detailed instructions from another file (or prompt for these instructions on the screen). The method of defining more than one set of input varies from one computer to another but it normally involves defining more variables to perform the input function.

The same is true of output. For example, the results of a program may be written to one file, but any error messages are displayed separately so that they do not contaminate the real data. Some implementations allow up to sixteen different input and output files or channels in one program.

11.2.3   Snobol on a Microcomputer

SNOBOL can be used on the IBM Personal Computer and some other microcomputers. The interpreter SNOBOL for the IBM PC can be obtained from

SNOBOL4
PO Box 441
Millwood
New York 10546

This implementation requires at least 192K of memory, with 256K or more recommended. It can use over 512K. Arithmetic on real numbers requires the 8087 coprocessor. It costs about $50.

SNOBOL4+ incorporates some extra functions, notably LPAD, RPAD, SORT and RSORT and runs on the IBM PC or other 8086/8088/80186/80126 processors which need not be compatible with the IBM PC. The machine must have PC or MS/DOS version 1.1 or above and a minimum of 128K memory. Up to approximately 448K of memory can be used with 192K recommended for programs of reasonable size. Real arithmetic can be done with or without the 8087. SNOBOL4+ is based on the Macro Implementation of SNOBOL4 for IBM370 and CDC7600 mainframes. The program is compiled into a compact internal notation which is then interpreted at execution time. SNOBOL4+ originated from

Catspaw Inc
PO Box 1123
Salida
Colorado 81201

and is now being marketed by Prentice-Hall together with a reference manual at a combined cost of $95.

More expensive at around \$200 is Macro SPITBOL for the IBM PC. This is a full implementation of Macro SPITBOL which needs 192K of memory on the IBM PC but should run on any machine supporting MS/DOS. This can be obtained from

Robert B. K. Dewar
SPITBOL Orders
74 5th Avenue
New York
NY 10003

Solutions to the Exercises

This appendix gives possible solutions to the exercises which appear at the end of each chapter. In many cases, there are several ways of solving a problem and the correct result may be obtained by a different method from that given here. These programs may also be considered as further examples.

The solutions to the exercises were run on a Digital VAX 11/780 using Macro SPITBOL, but features which are peculiar to SPITBOL are used only in the solutions to the exercises in Chapter 9. The program statistics which are printed before and after the results have different format in SNOBOL and in some other versions of SPITBOL.

1.1

```
          ************************************************************
          *
          *   Program to print out all the data with a blank line
          *   between each line
          *
          ************************************************************
          *
1             &STLIMIT = 10000
          *
          *   Read a line, print it then print a blank line
          *
2         MORE  LINE = INPUT      :F(END)
3               OUTPUT = LINE
4               OUTPUT =          :(MORE)
5         END


STORE USED        1411
STORE LEFT        24266
COMP ERRORS       0
REGENERATIONS     0
COMP TIME-MSEC    90
```


REMEMBER ME WHEN I AM GONE AWAY,

GONE FAR AWAY INTO THE SILENT LAND;

WHEN YOU CAN NO MORE HOLD ME BY THE HAND,

NOR I HALF TURN TO GO YET TURNING STAY.

REMEMBER ME WHEN NO MORE DAY BY DAY

YOU TELL ME OF OUR FUTURE THAT YOU PLANNED:

ONLY REMEMBER ME; YOU UNDERSTAND

IT WILL BE LATE TO COUNSEL THEN OR PRAY.

YET IF YOU SHOULD FORGET ME FOR A WHILE

AND AFTERWARDS REMEMBER, DO NOT GRIEVE:

FOR IF THE DARKNESS AND CORRUPTION LEAVE

A VESTIGE OF THE THOUGHTS THAT ONCE I HAD,

BETTER BY FAR YOU SHOULD FORGET AND SMILE

THAN THAT YOU SHOULD REMEMBER AND BE SAD.


```
NORMAL END
IN STATEMENT    5
RUN TIME-MSEC   40
STMTS EXECUTED 45
MCSEC / STMT    888
REGENERATIONS   0
```

The anchor is not set within this program as the program does not contain any pattern match statements. &TRIM is also unnecessary.

1.2

```
      *********************************************************
      *
      *    Program to print out all the lines which begin with
      *    REMEMBER
      *
      *********************************************************
      *
1            &STLIMIT = 10000
2            &ANCHOR = 1
3            &TRIM = 1
      *
      *    Read a line and print it if it begins with REMEMBER
      *
4     MORE   LINE = INPUT        :F(END)
5            LINE 'REMEMBER'     :F(MORE)
6            OUTPUT = LINE       :(MORE)
7     END
```

```
STORE USED     1415
STORE LEFT     24262
COMP ERRORS    0
REGENERATIONS  0
COMP TIME-MSEC 80
```

```
REMEMBER ME WHEN I AM GONE AWAY,
REMEMBER ME WHEN NO MORE DAY BY DAY


NORMAL END
IN STATEMENT    7
RUN TIME-MSEC   10
STMTS EXECUTED 35
MCSEC / STMT    285
REGENERATIONS   0
```

1.3

```
            *************************************************************
            *
            *   Program to print out all of the data changing each
            *   occurrence of REMEMBER to FORGET
            *
            *************************************************************
            *
1                   &STLIMIT = 10000
2                   &TRIM = 1
3                   &ANCHOR = 0
            *
            *   Read a line
            *
4           MORE  LINE = INPUT                       :F(END)
            *
            *   Change all occurrences of REMEMBER to FORGET then print
            *   line
            *
5           AGAIN LINE 'REMEMBER' = 'FORGET'     :S(AGAIN)
6                 OUTPUT = LINE                  :(MORE)
7           END


STORE USED       1419
STORE LEFT       24258
COMP ERRORS      0
REGENERATIONS    0
COMP TIME-MSEC  100


FORGET ME WHEN I AM GONE AWAY,
GONE FAR AWAY INTO THE SILENT LAND;
WHEN YOU CAN NO MORE HOLD ME BY THE HAND,
NOR I HALF TURN TO GO YET TURNING STAY.
FORGET ME WHEN NO MORE DAY BY DAY
YOU TELL ME OF OUR FUTURE THAT YOU PLANNED:
ONLY FORGET ME; YOU UNDERSTAND
IT WILL BE LATE TO COUNSEL THEN OR PRAY.
YET IF YOU SHOULD FORGET ME FOR A WHILE
```

AND AFTERWARDS FORGET, DO NOT GRIEVE:
FOR IF THE DARKNESS AND CORRUPTION LEAVE
A VESTIGE OF THE THOUGHTS THAT ONCE I HAD,
BETTER BY FAR YOU SHOULD FORGET AND SMILE
THAN THAT YOU SHOULD FORGET AND BE SAD.


```
NORMAL END
IN STATEMENT    7
RUN TIME-MSEC   50
STMTS EXECUTED 52
MCSEC / STMT    961
REGENERATIONS   0
```

1.4

```
         ***********************************************************
         *
         *   Program to print out every alternate line of data,
         *   deleting the spaces
         *
         ***********************************************************
         *
1              &STLIMIT = 10000
2              &ANCHOR = 0
3              &TRIM = 1
         *
         *   Read a line, delete spaces from it and print it
         *
4        MORE  LINE = INPUT      :F(END)
5        AGAIN LINE ' ' =        :S(AGAIN)
6              OUTPUT = LINE
         *
         *   Read next line to skip it
         *
7              LINE = INPUT      :S(MORE)
8        END
```


```
STORE USED      1414
STORE LEFT      24263
COMP ERRORS     0
REGENERATIONS   0
COMP TIME-MSEC 100
```


```
REMEMBERMEWHENIAMGONEAWAY,
WHENYOUCANNOMOREHOLDMEBYTHEHAND,
REMEMBERMEWHENNOMOREDAYBYDAY
ONLYREMEMBERME;YOUUNDERSTAND
YETIFYOUSHOULDFORGETMEFORAWHILE
FORIFTHEDARKNESSANDCORRUPTIONLEAVE
BETTERBYFARYOUSHOULDFORGETANDSMILE
```

```
NORMAL END
IN STATEMENT    8
RUN TIME-MSEC   60
STMTS EXECUTED 80
MCSEC / STMT    750
REGENERATIONS  0
```

There is no way in which SNOBOL can input only every alternate line. If a program is to omit some lines of data, it must input these lines but not process them any further. This is done by statement 7

```
        LINE = INPUT        :S(MORE)
```

which inputs a line then goes immediately to the statement labelled MORE to input another line, overwriting the one input by statement 7.

2.1

```
        ***********************************************************
        *
        *   Program to find all the people who were born in London
        *   or New York (codes LN or NY in columns 3 and 4)
        *
        ***********************************************************
        *
        *   Initialisation
        *
1           &STLIMIT = 10000
2           &TRIM = 1
3           &ANCHOR = 1
4           BIRTHPAT = 'LN' | 'NY'
        *
        *   Read a line and print it if it matches BIRTHPAT
        *
5   MORE  LINE = INPUT            :F(END)
6           LINE LEN(2) BIRTHPAT  :F(MORE)
7           OUTPUT = LINE         :(MORE)
8   END
```

```
STORE USED      1429
STORE LEFT      24248
COMP ERRORS     0
REGENERATIONS   0
COMP TIME-MSEC 110
```

```
 1LN1890062119531103LSMITH, JOHN*FRED
 2NY1900031519680122TBROWN, JAMES*WILLIAM
 4LN1908120119690115LWILSON, DAVID*JACK
 6NY1888072919621201JJAMES, KEITH*JOHN
 9NY1894091619490227DHARRIS, GEOFFREY*WILLIAM
11LN1899071319520819DMILES, JOSEPH*JOHN
13NY1906101519630829LEDWARDS, ALAN*HENRY
```

```
NORMAL END
IN STATEMENT    8
RUN TIME-MSEC   20
STMTS EXECUTED  41
MCSEC / STMT    487
REGENERATIONS   0
```

2.2

```
         **************************************************************
         *
         *    Program to find all the words which contain an L
         *
         **************************************************************
         *
         *    Initialisation
         *
1             &STLIMIT = 10000
2             &TRIM = 1
3             &ANCHOR = 1
4             LETTERS = 'ABCDEFGHIJKLMNOPQRSTUVWXYZ'
5             WORDPAT = BREAK(LETTERS) SPAN(LETTERS) . WORD
         *
         *    Read a line
         *
6        MORE  LINE = INPUT        :F(END)
         *
         *    Extract words and print those containing L
         *
7        AGAIN LINE WORDPAT =      :F(MORE)
8              WORD BREAK('L')     :F(AGAIN)
9              OUTPUT = WORD       :(AGAIN)
10       END
```

```
STORE USED      1423
STORE LEFT      24254
COMP ERRORS     0
REGENERATIONS   0
COMP TIME-MSEC  120
```

```
SILENT
LAND
HOLD
HALF
TELL
PLANNED
ONLY
WILL
LATE
COUNSEL
SHOULD
```

```
WHILE
LEAVE
SHOULD
SMILE
SHOULD


NORMAL END
IN STATEMENT    10
RUN TIME-MSEC   110
STMTS EXECUTED 273
MCSEC / STMT    402
REGENERATIONS  0
```

2.3

```
          ************************************************************
          *
          *   Program to find all the people who were born in
          *   London (LN in columns 3 and 4) or who were lawyers
          *   (L in column 21)
          *
          ************************************************************
          *
          *   Initialisation
          *
1             &TRIM = 1
2             &STLIMIT = 10000
3             &ANCHOR = 1
4             PAT1 = LEN(2) 'LN'
5             PAT2 = LEN(20) 'L'
6             PAT = PAT1 | PAT2
          *
          *   Read a line and print it if it matches PAT
          *
7     MORE  LINE = INPUT        :F(END)
8           LINE PAT            :F(MORE)
9           OUTPUT = LINE       :(MORE)
10    END
```

```
STORE USED      1426
STORE LEFT      24251
COMP ERRORS     0
REGENERATIONS   0
COMP TIME-MSEC 130
```

```
 1LN1890062119531103LSMITH, JOHN*FRED
 4LN1908120119690115LWILSON, DAVID*JACK
 8SY1902110419480915LGREEN, GEORGE*FRED
10T01903052919600205LROBERTS, DAVID*WILLIAM
11LN1899071319520819DMILES, JOSEPH*JOHN
13NY1906101519630829LEDWARDS, ALAN*HENRY
```

```
NORMAL END
IN STATEMENT    10
RUN TIME-MSEC   20
STMTS EXECUTED 42
MCSEC / STMT    476
REGENERATIONS   0
```

2.4

```
         ************************************************************
         *
         *   Program to print out the people file with spaces between
         *   the fields. The father's name is omitted
         *
         ************************************************************
         *
         *   Initialisation
         *
1            &STLIMIT = 10000
2            &TRIM = 1
3            &ANCHOR = 1
4            SP = ' '
5            BREAKUP = LEN(2) . IDEN LEN(2) . PLACE LEN(8) . BIRTH
         + LEN(8) . DEATH LEN(1) . JOB BREAK('*') . NAME
         *
         *   Read data and extract fields
         *
6    MORE    LINE = INPUT        :F(END)
7            LINE BREAKUP
         *
         *   Print data with spaces between the fields
         *
8            OUTPUT = IDEN SP PLACE SP BIRTH SP DEATH SP JOB SP
         + NAME               :(MORE)
9    END
```

```
STORE USED      1468
STORE LEFT      24209
COMP ERRORS     0
REGENERATIONS   0
COMP TIME-MSEC 130
```

```
1  LN  18900621  19531103  L  SMITH, JOHN
2  NY  19000315  19680122  T  BROWN, JAMES
3  SY  18980409  19520628  A  JONES, HENRY
4  LN  19081201  19690115  L  WILSON, DAVID
5  ED  18980312  19560902  J  SCOTT, MICHAEL
6  NY  18880729  19621201  J  JAMES, KEITH
7  CH  18990131  19521029  D  WILLIAMS, PETER
8  SY  19021104  19480915  L  GREEN, GEORGE
9  NY  18940916  19490227  D  HARRIS, GEOFFREY
```

```
10  TO  19030529  19600205  L  ROBERTS, DAVID
11  LN  18990713  19520819  D  MILES, JOSEPH
12  TO  19020603  19690429  J  WHITE, PETER
13  NY  19061015  19630829  L  EDWARDS, ALAN
14  CH  18981114  19591013  A  PETERSON, WILLIAM
```

```
NORMAL END
IN STATEMENT    9
RUN TIME-MSEC   70
STMTS EXECUTED  49
MCSEC / STMT    1428
REGENERATIONS   0
```

The pattern BREAKUP is used to separate out the fields into different variables. In the OUTPUT statement they are concatenated again with spaces between them. The variable SP is used to store the spaces as only it need be changed if a different number of spaces is required.

2.5

```
            ***********************************************************
            *
            *   Program to print each line of its data backwards
            *
            ***********************************************************
            *
1               &STLIMIT = 10000
2               &ANCHOR = 1
3               &TRIM = 1
            *
            *   Read a line
            *
4       MORE  LINE = INPUT              :F(END)
            *
            *   Take letters from line one by one and concatenate them
            *   into BACK
            *
5       AGAIN LINE LEN(1) . CH =        :F(PRINT)
6             BACK = CH BACK            :(AGAIN)
            *
            *   End of line. Print BACK and clear it for next line
            *
7       PRINT OUTPUT = BACK
8             BACK =                    :(MORE)
9       END
```

```
STORE USED      1420
STORE LEFT      24257
COMP ERRORS     0
REGENERATIONS   0
COMP TIME-MSEC  110
```

```
,YAWA ENOG MA I NEHW EM REBMEMER
;DNAL TNELIS EHT OTNI YAWA RAF ENOG
,DNAH EHT YB EM DLOH EROM ON NAC UOY NEHW
.YATS GNINRUT TEY OG OT NRUT FLAH I RON
YAD YB YAD EROM ON NEHW EM REBMEMER
:DENNALP UOY TAHT ERUTUF RUO FO EM LLET UOY
DNATSREDNU UOY ;EM REBMEMER YLNO
.YARP RO NEHT LESNUOC OT ETAL EB LLIW TI
ELIHW A ROF EM TEGROF DLUOHS UOY FI TEY
:EVEIRG TON OD ,REBMEMER SDRAWRETFA DNA
EVAEL NOITPURROC DNA SSENKRAD EHT FI ROF
,DAH I ECNO TAHT STHGUOHT EHT FO EGITSEV A
ELIMS DNA TEGROF DLUOHS UOY RAF YB RETTEB
.DAS EB DNA REBMEMER DLUOHS UOY TAHT NAHT
```

```
NORMAL END
IN STATEMENT   9
RUN TIME-MSEC   350
STMTS EXECUTED 1139
MCSEC / STMT   307
REGENERATIONS  0
```

The statement

```
AGAIN LINE LEN(1) . CH =     :F(PRINT)
```

takes the first character from LINE and puts it into CH. BACK is initially a null string. The first time that

```
      BACK = CH BACK        :(AGAIN)
```

is executed BACK contains R (the first R of REMEMBER). LINE is now

```
EMBER ME WHEN I AM GONE AWAY,
```

The program loops back to AGAIN and takes the next character from LINE, the E. This is concatenated on to the beginning of BACK so that BACK now contains ER. Successive characters are taken from LINE and the line is built up backwards in BACK. When there are no more characters left in LINE, BACK is printed and then set to the null string by

```
      BACK =                :(MORE)
```

before the next line is input.

3.1
```
      ************************************************************
      *
      *  Program to count the total number of words in the sonnet
      *
      ************************************************************
      *
      *  Initialisation
      *
1          &STLIMIT = 10000
2          &ANCHOR = 1
3          &TRIM = 1
```

```
4                LETTERS = 'ABCDEFGHIJKLMNOPQRSTUVWXYZ'
5                WORDPAT = BREAK(LETTERS) SPAN(LETTERS)
        *
        *  Read a line
        *
6       MORE  LINE = INPUT        :F(PRINT)
        *
        *  Get words and count them
        *
7       NEXT  LINE WORDPAT =      :F(MORE)
8             COUNT = COUNT + 1 :(NEXT)
        *
        *  End of input - print result
        *
9       PRINT OUTPUT = 'THE NUMBER OF WORDS IN THE SONNET IS ' COUNT

10      END
```

```
STORE USED       1432
STORE LEFT       24245
COMP ERRORS      0
REGENERATIONS    0
COMP TIME-MSEC 160
```

```
THE NUMBER OF WORDS IN THE SONNET IS 111
```

```
NORMAL END
IN STATEMENT     10
RUN TIME-MSEC    70
STMTS EXECUTED 258
MCSEC / STMT    271
REGENERATIONS    0
```

The words are only counted, not inspected individually and so there is no need to assign each word to a variable.

3.2

```
        ***********************************************************
        *
        *  Program to calculate the percentage of people who were
        *  lawyers
        *
        ***********************************************************
        *
        *  Initialisation
        *
1               &ANCHOR = 1
2               &TRIM = 1
3               &STLIMIT = 10000
4               LAWYER = LEN(20) 'L'
```

```
       *
       *   Count total number of people and number of lawyers
       *
5      MORE   LINE = INPUT                  :F(PRINT)
6             TOTAL = TOTAL + 1
7             LINE LAWYER                   :F(MORE)
8             LAWYERS = LAWYERS + 1    :(MORE)
       *
       *   Calculate percentage and print result
       *
9      PRINT PERC = 100.0 * LAWYERS / TOTAL
10            OUTPUT = 'LAWYERS WERE ' PERC '% OF THE PEOPLE'
11     END
```

```
STORE USED      1431
STORE LEFT      24246
COMP ERRORS     0
REGENERATIONS   0
COMP TIME-MSEC 140
```

```
LAWYERS WERE 35.7143% OF THE PEOPLE
```

```
NORMAL END
IN STATEMENT    11
RUN TIME-MSEC   20
STMTS EXECUTED 55
MCSEC / STMT   363
REGENERATIONS   0
```

3.3

```
       ************************************************************
       *
       *   Program to count the number of people who were 60 or
       *   more at death
       *
       ************************************************************
       *
       *   Initialisation
       *
1             &STLIMIT = 10000
2             &TRIM = 1
3             &ANCHOR = 1
4             DATES = LEN(4) LEN(8) . BIRTH LEN(8) . DEATH
       *
       *   Read data and extract dates
       *
5      MORE   LINE = INPUT                  :F(PRINT)
6             LINE DATES
       *
       *   Count if difference is 60 years or more
       *
7             LT(DEATH - BIRTH,600000)      :S(MORE)
8             COUNT = COUNT + 1             :(MORE)
```

```
           *
           *  Print result
           *
9          PRINT OUTPUT = 'NUMBER OF PEOPLE WHO WERE 60 OR MORE '
           +  'AT DEATH IS ' COUNT
10         END
```

```
STORE USED       1451
STORE LEFT       24226
COMP ERRORS      0
REGENERATIONS    0
COMP TIME-MSEC   140
```

```
NUMBER OF PEOPLE WHO WERE 60 OR MORE AT DEATH IS 6
```

```
NORMAL END
IN STATEMENT     10
RUN TIME-MSEC    30
STMTS EXECUTED   55
MCSEC / STMT     545
REGENERATIONS    0
```

The age is found by subtracting the date of birth from the date of death. The program needs to allow for the whole of each date, not just the year. A man born on 3 November 1902 i.e. 19021103 and dying on 2 March 1962 i.e. 19620302 would be considered to be 60 if only the years were allowed for and 1902 was subtracted from 1962, even though he was only 59. To get the correct result, the whole of each date is treated as one big number. It does not matter that the fifth and sixth digits can never be more than 12 or the seventh and eighth never more than 31. The subtraction for a man born on 3 November 1902 and dying on 4 November 1962 is 19621104 − 19021103, giving 600001 and so a difference of 600000 or more indicates that he has reached his sixtieth birthday.

3.4

```
        ***********************************************************
        *
        *  Program to print out all the words in the first
        *  ten lines of data which contain R
        *
        ***********************************************************
        *
        *  Initialisation
        *
1          &ANCHOR = 1
2          &TRIM = 1
3          &STLIMIT = 10000
4          LETTERS = 'ABCDEFGHIJKLMNOPQRSTUVWXYZ'
5          WORDPAT = BREAK(LETTERS) SPAN(LETTERS) . WORD
```

```
       *
       *   Test for 10 lines done - if not, read another one
       *
6      MORE  LINES = LT(LINES,10) LINES + 1       :F(END)
7            LINE = INPUT                         :F(END)
       *
       *   Look for word containing R and print it
       *
8      AGAIN LINE WORDPAT =                :F(MORE)
9            WORD BREAK('R')               :F(AGAIN)
10           OUTPUT = WORD                 :(AGAIN)
11     END
```

```
STORE USED      1425
STORE LEFT      24252
COMP ERRORS     0
REGENERATIONS   0
COMP TIME-MSEC 100
```

```
REMEMBER
FAR
MORE
NOR
TURN
TURNING
REMEMBER
MORE
OUR
FUTURE
REMEMBER
UNDERSTAND
OR
PRAY
FORGET
FOR
AFTERWARDS
REMEMBER
GRIEVE
```

```
NORMAL END
IN STATEMENT    11
RUN TIME-MSEC   80
STMTS EXECUTED 214
MCSEC / STMT   373
REGENERATIONS   0
```

4.1

```
          **********************************************************
          *
          *   Program to count the number of occurrences of the word
          *   YOU
          *
          **********************************************************
          *
          *   Initialisation
          *
1                 &ANCHOR = 1
2                 &TRIM = 1
3                 &STLIMIT = 10000
4                 LETTERS = 'ABCDEFGHIJKLMNOPQRSTUVWXYZ'
5                 WORDPAT = BREAK(LETTERS) SPAN(LETTERS) . WORD
          *
          *   Read data and look for YOU
          *
6         NEXT  LINE = INPUT          :F(PRINT)
7         AGAIN LINE WORDPAT =        :F(NEXT)
8               IDENT(WORD,'YOU')     :F(AGAIN)
9               COUNT = COUNT + 1     :(AGAIN)
          *
          *   Print result
          *
10        PRINT OUTPUT = DUPL(' ',10) 'Number of occurrences of YOU '
          + 'is ' COUNT
11        END
```

```
STORE USED      1438
STORE LEFT      24239
COMP ERRORS     0
REGENERATIONS   0
COMP TIME-MSEC 140
```

```
          Number of occurrences of YOU is 7
```

```
NORMAL END
IN STATEMENT    11
RUN TIME-MSEC   80
STMTS EXECUTED 265
MCSEC / STMT    301
REGENERATIONS   0
```

4.2

```
        *****************************************************
        *
        *   Program to find words which end in S or Y
        *
        *****************************************************
        *
        *   Initialisation
        *
1             &ANCHOR = 1
2             &TRIM = 1
3             &STLIMIT = 10000
4             LETTERS = 'ABCDEFGHIJKLMNOPQRSTUVWXYZ'
5             WORDPAT = BREAK(LETTERS) SPAN(LETTERS) . WORD
        *
        *   Read data and look for words ending in S or Y
        *
6       MORE  LINE = INPUT               :F(END)
7       AGAIN LINE WORDPAT =             :F(MORE)
8             WORD RTAB(1) ANY('SY')     :F(AGAIN)
9             OUTPUT = WORD              :(AGAIN)
10      END
```

```
STORE USED      1684
STORE LEFT      23993
COMP ERRORS     0
REGENERATIONS   0
COMP TIME-MSEC 120
```

```
AWAY
AWAY
BY
STAY
DAY
BY
DAY
ONLY
PRAY
AFTERWARDS
DARKNESS
THOUGHTS
BY
```

```
NORMAL END
IN STATEMENT    10
RUN TIME-MSEC   100
STMTS EXECUTED 270
MCSEC / STMT    370
REGENERATIONS   0
```

4.3

```
      ***********************************************************
      *
      *   Program to print out the names and identification
      *   numbers of the people with the names reformatted to
      *   upper and lower case
      *
      ***********************************************************
      *
      *   Initialisation
      *
1         &ANCHOR = 1
2         &TRIM = 1
3         &STLIMIT = 10000
4         PAT = LEN(2) . IDEN LEN(19) BREAK(',') . SNAME
   +   SPAN(' ,') BREAK('*') . CNAME
5         UPPERS = 'ABCDEFGHIJKLMNOPQRSTUVWXYZ'
6         LOWERS = 'abcdefghijklmnopqrstuvwxyz'
      *
      *   Read data and extract names and numbers
      *
7  MORE   LINE = INPUT        :F(END)
8         LINE PAT
      *
      *   Reformat names and output them
      *
9         CNAME LEN(1) . C REM . CNAME
10        SNAME LEN(1) . S REM . SNAME
11        OUTPUT = IDEN '  ' C REPLACE(CNAME,UPPERS,LOWERS) ' '
   +   S REPLACE(SNAME,UPPERS,LOWERS)        :(MORE)
12 END
```

```
STORE USED      1760
STORE LEFT      23917
COMP ERRORS     0
REGENERATIONS   0
COMP TIME-MSEC 160
```

```
 1  John Smith
 2  James Brown
 3  Henry Jones
 4  David Wilson
 5  Michael Scott
 6  Keith James
 7  Peter Williams
 8  George Green
 9  Geoffrey Harris
10  David Roberts
11  Joseph Miles
12  Peter White
13  Alan Edwards
14  William Peterson
```

```
NORMAL END
IN STATEMENT    12
RUN TIME-MSEC   60
STMTS EXECUTED  78
MCSEC / STMT    769
REGENERATIONS   0
```

4.4

```
         ***********************************************************
         *
         *   Program to find the word which comes first in
         *   alphabetical order in each line
         *
         ***********************************************************
         *
         *   Initialisation
         *
1            &STLIMIT = 10000
2            &TRIM = 1
3            &ANCHOR = 1
4            LETTERS = 'ABCDEFGHIJKLMNOPQRSTUVWXYZ'
5            WORDPAT = BREAK(LETTERS) SPAN(LETTERS) . NEXTWORD
         *
         *   Read line and get first word to start off comparisons
         *
6    MORE  LINE = INPUT          :F(END)
7          LINE BREAK(LETTERS) SPAN(LETTERS) . WORD =
         *
         *   Test alphabetical order with successive words
         *
8    AGAIN LINE WORDPAT =        :F(PRINT)
9          LGT(NEXTWORD,WORD)    :S(AGAIN)
10         WORD = NEXTWORD       :(AGAIN)
         *
         *   Print result
         *
11   PRINT OUTPUT = WORD         :(MORE)
12   END
```

```
STORE USED      1420
STORE LEFT      24257
COMP ERRORS     0
REGENERATIONS   0
COMP TIME-MSEC 140
```

```
AM
AWAY
BY
GO
BY
FUTURE
ME
```

```
BE
A
AFTERWARDS
AND
A
AND
AND


NORMAL END
IN STATEMENT    12
RUN TIME-MSEC   110
STMTS EXECUTED 286
MCSEC / STMT    384
REGENERATIONS   0
```

Statement 7 puts the first word into WORD to start off the comparisons. Statement 8 puts the second word into NEXTWORD and the two are compared by

```
        LGT(NEXTWORD,WORD)    :S(AGAIN)
```

If NEXTWORD is earlier in the alphabet it is put into WORD. The third word is then put into NEXTWORD and compared with WORD. If the third word is earlier in the alphabet it is put into WORD. Thus each new word is put into NEXTWORD and compared with WORD which holds the one we have found so far. WORD is printed when the end of the line is reached. For the first line of the sonnet WORD is successively REMEMBER, ME, I, AM. For the second line it is GONE, FAR, AWAY.

5.1

```
            *************************************************************
            *
            *   Program to make a word count of all words which begin
            *   with R, S or T
            *
            *************************************************************
            *
            *   Initialisation
            *
1                   &STLIMIT = 10000
2                   &ANCHOR = 1
3                   &TRIM = 1
4                   LETTERS = 'ABCDEFGHIJKLMNOPQRSTUVWXYZ'
5                   WORDPAT = BREAK(LETTERS) SPAN(LETTERS) . WORD
6                   COUNT = TABLE()
            *
            *   Read a line
            *
7           READ  LINE = INPUT        :F(PRINT)
            *
            *   Count words beginning with R, S or T
            *
8           NEXT  LINE WORDPAT =      :F(READ)
9                 WORD ANY('RST')     :F(NEXT)
10                COUNT<WORD> = COUNT<WORD> + 1      :(NEXT)
```

```
           *
           *   Print results - first the heading
           *
11         PRINT HEAD = 'COUNT OF WORDS BEGINNING WITH R, S OR T'
12               OUTPUT = HEAD
13               OUTPUT = DUPL('-',SIZE(HEAD))
14               OUTPUT =
           *
           *   Convert table to an array and print it
           *
15               COUNT = CONVERT(COUNT,'ARRAY')             :F(EMPTY)
16               I = 1
17         AGAIN OUTPUT = COUNT<I,1> ' = ' COUNT<I,2>   :F(END)
18               I = I + 1          :(AGAIN)
           *
           *   Error message for empty table
           *
19         EMPTY OUTPUT = 'NO WORDS FOUND'
20         END
```

```
STORE USED       1709
STORE LEFT       23968
COMP ERRORS      0
REGENERATIONS    0
COMP TIME-MSEC 200
```

```
COUNT OF WORDS BEGINNING WITH R, S OR T
----------------------------------------

SILENT = 1
TELL = 1
THEN = 1
SHOULD = 3
SAD = 1
THAN = 1
STAY = 1
TO = 2
TURNING = 1
THAT = 3
THOUGHTS = 1
REMEMBER = 5
THE = 4
TURN = 1
SMILE = 1
```

```
NORMAL END
IN STATEMENT    20
RUN TIME-MSEC  130
STMTS EXECUTED 322
MCSEC / STMT   403
REGENERATIONS   0
```

Note how the heading is underlined. The variable HEAD is set to the text of the heading which is printed by

        OUTPUT = HEAD

The statement

        OUTPUT = DUPL('-',SIZE(HEAD))

prints a line of minus signs underneath the heading. SIZE(HEAD) ensures that the correct number of minus signs is printed.

5.2

```
        **********************************************************
        *
        *   Program to count the number of people from each
        *   occupation
        *
        **********************************************************
        *
        *   Initialisation
        *
1              &STLIMIT = 10000
2              &ANCHOR = 1
3              &TRIM = 1
4              COUNT = TABLE()
5              FINDJOB = LEN(20) LEN(1) . JOB
        *
        *   Read a line and count occupation
        *
6       MORE  LINE = INPUT                      :F(PRINT)
7             LINE FINDJOB
8             COUNT<JOB> = COUNT<JOB> + 1    :(MORE)
        *
        *   Print totals
        *
9       PRINT COUNT = CONVERT(COUNT,'ARRAY')       :F(EMPTY)
10            OUTPUT = 'Count of Occupations'
11            OUTPUT =
12            I = 1
13      AGAIN OUTPUT = COUNT<I,1> ' = ' COUNT<I,2>  :F(END)
14            I  = I + 1     :(AGAIN)
        *
        *   Error message for empty table
        *
15      EMPTY OUTPUT = 'No Occupations Found'
16      END


STORE USED      1444
STORE LEFT      24233
COMP ERRORS     0
REGENERATIONS   0
COMP TIME-MSEC  120
```

```
Count of Occupations

A = 2
J = 3
T = 1
D = 3
L = 5


NORMAL END
IN STATEMENT    16
RUN TIME-MSEC   40
STMTS EXECUTED  64
MCSEC / STMT    625
REGENERATIONS   0
```

5.3

```
         ************************************************************
         *
         *   Program to count the number of people from each
         *   occupation, printing the names of the occupations
         *
         ************************************************************
         *
         *   Initialisation
         *
1            &STLIMIT = 10000
2            &ANCHOR = 1
3            &TRIM = 1
4            JOBS = TABLE(5)
5            JOBS<'A'> = 'Accountant'
6            JOBS<'D'> = 'Doctor'
7            JOBS<'J'> = 'Journalist'
8            JOBS<'L'> = 'Lawyer'
9            JOBS<'T'> = 'Teacher'
10           COUNT = TABLE()
11           FINDJOB = LEN(20) LEN(1) . JOB
         *
         *   Read a line and count occupation
         *
12   MORE  LINE = INPUT                        :F(PRINT)
13           LINE FINDJOB
14           COUNT<JOB> = COUNT<JOB> + 1    :(MORE)
         *
         *   Print totals
         *
15   PRINT COUNT = CONVERT(COUNT,'ARRAY')                  :F(EMPTY)
16           OUTPUT = 'Count of Occupations'
17           OUTPUT =
18           I = 1
19   AGAIN OUTPUT = JOBS<COUNT<I,1>> ' = ' COUNT<I,2>  :F(END)
20           I = I + 1     :(AGAIN)
         *
         *   Error message for empty table
         *
21   EMPTY OUTPUT = 'No Occupations Found'
22           END
```

```
STORE USED      1483
STORE LEFT      24194
COMP ERRORS     0
REGENERATIONS   0
COMP TIME-MSEC 180


Count of Occupations

Accountant = 2
Journalist = 3
Teacher = 1
Doctor = 3
Lawyer = 5


NORMAL END
IN STATEMENT     22
RUN TIME-MSEC    40
STMTS EXECUTED  70
MCSEC / STMT    571
REGENERATIONS   0
```

The abbreviations are used as subscripts to the table COUNT when the occupations are counted. JOBS<COUNT<I,1>> is the full name of the occupation. The contents of element I,1 of the array COUNT are used as the subscript to the table JOBS. If COUNT<I,1> is L, JOBS<COUNT<I,1>> is Lawyer.

5.4

```
          ***********************************************************
          *      |
          *   Program to print out the identification numbers,
          *   names and dates of birth
          *
          ***********************************************************
          *
          *   Initialisation
          *
1             &STLIMIT = 10000
2             &ANCHOR = 1
3             &TRIM = 1
          *
4             MONTHS = TABLE()
5             MONTHS<'01'> = 'January'
6             MONTHS<'02'> = 'February'
7             MONTHS<'03'> = 'March'
8             MONTHS<'04'> = 'April'
9             MONTHS<'05'> = 'May'
10            MONTHS<'06'> = 'June'
11            MONTHS<'07'> = 'July'
12            MONTHS<'08'> = 'August'
13            MONTHS<'09'> = 'September'
14            MONTHS<'10'> = 'October'
```

```
15              MONTHS<'11'> = 'November'
16              MONTHS<'12'> = 'December'
        *
17              UPPERS = 'ABCDEFGHIJKLMNOPQRSTUVWXYZ'
18              LOWERS = 'abcdefghijklmnopqrstuvwxyz'
19              SPLIT = LEN(2) . IDEN LEN(2) LEN(4) . YEAR LEN(2) .
     +  MONTH LEN(2) . DAY LEN(9) BREAK('*') . NAME
        *
        *  Output headings
        *
20              OUTPUT = '  IDEN   NAME' DUPL(' ',21)
     +  'DATE OF BIRTH'
21              OUTPUT =
        *
        *  Read a line and extract fields
        *
22      MORE   LINE = INPUT      :F(END)
23              LINE SPLIT
        *
        *  Reformat name and date and print them
        *
24              NAME LEN(1) . S BREAK(',') . SNAME SPAN(', ') . GAP
     +  LEN(1) . C  REM . CNAME
25              DAY '0' = ' '
        *
26              OUTPUT = DUPL(' ',4) IDEN ' ' S
     +  REPLACE(SNAME,UPPERS,LOWERS) GAP C
     +  REPLACE(CNAME,UPPERS,LOWERS) DUPL(' ',25 - SIZE(NAME))
     +  DAY ' ' MONTHS<MONTH> ' ' YEAR   :(MORE)
27      END
```

```
STORE USED       1905
STORE LEFT       23772
COMP ERRORS      0
REGENERATIONS    0
COMP TIME-MSEC   250
```

IDEN	NAME	DATE OF BIRTH
1	Smith, John	21 June 1890
2	Brown, James	15 March 1900
3	Jones, Henry	9 April 1898
4	Wilson, David	1 December 1908
5	Scott, Michael	12 March 1898
6	James, Keith	29 July 1888
7	Williams, Peter	31 January 1899
8	Green, George	4 November 1902
9	Harris, Geoffrey	16 September 1894
10	Roberts, David	29 May 1903
11	Miles, Joseph	13 July 1899
12	White, Peter	3 June 1902
13	Edwards, Alan	15 October 1906
14	Peterson, William	14 November 1898

```
NORMAL END
IN STATEMENT    27
RUN TIME-MSEC   110
STMTS EXECUTED 93
MCSEC / STMT   1182
REGENERATIONS   0
```

Even though they are digits, the table subscripts are strings and so must be enclosed in quotes. DUPL(' ',25 - SIZE(NAME)) calculates how many spaces are required after the name to make the dates line up in a column. The names are converted to upper and lower case.

6.1

```
        **********************************************************
        *
        *   Program to make a word count of all words beginning with
        *   a vowel and all words ending with a vowel
        *
        **********************************************************
        *
        *   Initialisation
        *
1           &STLIMIT = 10000
2           &ANCHOR = 1
3           &TRIM = 1
4           VOWELB = TABLE()
5           VOWELE = TABLE()
6           LETTERS = 'ABCDEFGHIJKLMNOPQRSTUVWXYZ'
7           NEXTW = BREAK(LETTERS) SPAN(LETTERS) . WORD
        *
8           DEFINE('PRINT(FREQ,TYPE,TOT)I,J,L,HEADING,TEXT')
        *
        *   Read text
        *
9    MORE   LINE = INPUT                :F(OUT)
10   AGAIN  LINE NEXTW =                :F(MORE)
        *
        *   Find words beginning with a vowel
        *
11          WORD ANY('AEIOU')          :F(TRY)
12          VOWELB<WORD> = VOWELB<WORD> + 1
        *
        *   Hold total of words beginning with a vowel in BEGTOT
        *
13          BEGTOT = BEGTOT + 1
        *
        *   Find words ending with a vowel
        *
14   TRY    WORD RTAB(1) ANY('AEIOU')       :F(AGAIN)
15          VOWELE<WORD> = VOWELE<WORD> + 1
        *
        *   Hold total of words ending with a vowel in ENDTOT
        *
16          ENDTOT = ENDTOT + 1              :(AGAIN)
        *
        *   Print words beginning with a vowel
        *
```

```
17     OUT    OUTPUT =
18            PRINT(VOWELB,'beginning',BEGTOT)
       *
       *   Print words ending with a vowel
       *
19            OUTPUT =
20            OUTPUT =
21            PRINT(VOWELE,'ending',ENDTOT)   :(END)
       *
       *   Function PRINT(FREQ,TYPE,TOT) prints table FREQ and
       *   total TOT. TYPE is used in the heading
       *
22     PRINT
23            HEADING = 'Count of words ' TYPE ' with a vowel'
       *
       *   Table is converted to an array for output
       *
24            FREQ = CONVERT(FREQ,'ARRAY')     :F(PRINT.ERR)
       *
       *   Print heading in centre of page which is 72 characters
       *   wide
       *
25            L = (72 - SIZE(HEADING)) / 2
26            OUTPUT = DUPL(' ',L) HEADING
27            OUTPUT = DUPL(' ',L) DUPL('-',SIZE(HEADING))
28            OUTPUT =
       *
       *   Print the words in columns together with their frequency
       *
29               I = 1
30     PRINT.1  J = 1
31     PRINT.2  TEXT = TEXT FREQ<I,2> '  ' FREQ<I,1>
     +    DUPL(' ',14 - SIZE(FREQ<I,1>))         :F(PRINT.3)
32               I = I + 1
33               J = LT(J,4) J + 1               :S(PRINT.2)
34               OUTPUT = TEXT
35               TEXT =                          :(PRINT.1)
36     PRINT.3  OUTPUT = TEXT
37               OUTPUT =
       *
       *   Print totals. The value of I is now one greater than
       *   the number of different words
       *
38               OUTPUT = 'Total number of words ' TYPE ' with a '
     +    'vowel is ' TOT
39               OUTPUT = 'Number of different words ' TYPE ' with '
     +    'a vowel is ' I - 1                 :(RETURN)
       *
       *   Error message if no words found
       *
40     PRINT.ERR  OUTPUT = 'No words ' TYPE ' with a vowel found '
     +                                :(RETURN)
41     PRINT.END
42     END
```

```
STORE USED      1793
STORE LEFT      23884
COMP ERRORS     0
REGENERATIONS   0
COMP TIME-MSEC 320
```

Count of words beginning with a vowel

1	INTO	2	IF	4	AND	2	A
1	ONLY	1	IT	2	AWAY	3	I
1	OR	1	UNDERSTAND	1	ONCE	1	OUR
1	AM	2	OF	1	AFTERWARDS		

Total number of words beginning with a vowel is 24
Number of different words beginning with a vowel is 15

Count of words ending with a vowel

1	INTO	1	DO	1	VESTIGE	2	GONE
1	GO	2	A	2	MORE	2	BE
3	I	2	NO	1	GRIEVE	2	TO
1	FUTURE	1	LATE	7	YOU	1	ONCE
1	LEAVE	6	ME	4	THE	1	WHILE
1	SMILE						

Total number of words ending with a vowel is 43
Number of different words ending with a vowel is 21

```
NORMAL END
IN STATEMENT     42
RUN TIME-MSEC    250
STMTS EXECUTED  670
MCSEC / STMT    373
REGENERATIONS    0
```

The statement

```
L = (72 - SIZE(HEADING)) / 2
```

calculates how many spaces are needed before the heading to centre it on a 72-character line. If L is an odd number, the integer division causes one less space before the heading than after it.

The words are printed in four columns and DUPL(' ',14 - SIZE(FREQ<I,1>)) calculates the number of spaces to be printed after the word so that the next column lines up. If the numbers are likely to be greater than 9, an appropriate number of spaces must also be inserted before them. The SPITBOL functions LPAD and RPAD provide a much more convenient way of doing this.

In function PRINT, successive pairs of frequencies and words are concatenated into TEXT from FREQ until J becomes 4 indicating that four columns have been built up. TEXT is then printed and emptied before the next four are put into it. At the end of the array, unless the number of elements is exactly divisible by 4, there will be an incomplete line in TEXT. This is printed by

```
PRINT.3  OUTPUT = TEXT
```

A blank line is printed by this statement if the last line was not incomplete.

6.2

```
        ************************************************************
        *
        *  Program to validate the people data, checking
        *  occupations, places of birth and names
        *
        ************************************************************
        *
        *  Initialisation
        *
1              &STLIMIT = 10000
2              &ANCHOR = 1
3              &TRIM = 1
4              DEFINE('CHECK(FIELD,CODES,TEXT)')
        *
5              PLACES = 'CH' | 'ED' | 'LN' | 'NY' | 'SY' | 'TO'
6              JOBS = ANY('ADJLT')
7              NAMELETS = 'ABCDEFGHIJKLMNOPQRSTUVWXYZ'
8              NAMES = SPAN(NAMELETS) SPAN(', ') SPAN(NAMELETS)
        +  RPOS(0)
        *
9              SPLIT = LEN(2) LEN(2) . PLACE LEN(16) LEN(1) . JOB
        +  BREAK('*') . NAME
        *
        *  Read a line and extract fields
        *
10     MORE  LINE = INPUT       :F(END)
11             LINE SPLIT
        *
        *  Check place, occupation and name
        *
12             CHECK(PLACE,PLACES,LINE)
13             CHECK(JOB,JOBS,LINE)
14             CHECK(NAME,NAMES,LINE)        :(MORE)
        *
        *  Function CHECK(FIELD,CODES,TEXT) checks field called
        *  FIELD for code called CODE.  TEXT is the input line
        *
15     CHECK FIELD CODES                     :S(RETURN)
        *
        *  Error message if wrong
        *
16             OUTPUT =
```

```
17              OUTPUT = TEXT
18              OUTPUT = ' *** Above line is erroneous'
19              OUTPUT = ' *** Field is ' FIELD          :(RETURN)
20      CHECK.END
21      END
```

```
STORE USED      1795
STORE LEFT      23882
COMP ERRORS     0
REGENERATIONS   0
COMP TIME-MSEC 190
```

```
15CN1890062119531103LSMITH, JOHN*FRED
 *** Above line is erroneous
 *** Field is CN

16NY1900031519680122SBROWN, JAMES*WILLIAM
 *** Above line is erroneous
 *** Field is S

17SY1898040919520628AJONES: HENRY*PETER
 *** Above line is erroneous
 *** Field is JONES: HENRY
```

```
NORMAL END
IN STATEMENT    21
RUN TIME-MSEC   50
STMTS EXECUTED 159
MCSEC / STMT    314
REGENERATIONS   0
```

For this program some extra data lines have been added which are erroneous. Function CHECK is written in such a way that it need not be altered if more items to be checked are added. Each new item needs a pattern against which is it matched.

7.1

```
*********************************************************
*
*    Program to underline all occurrences of the letter T
*
*********************************************************
*
*    Initialisation
*
1              &STLIMIT = 10000
2              &TRIM = 1
3              &ANCHOR = 1
*
*    Read a line and print it
*
4       MORE   LINE = INPUT     :F(END)
5              OUTPUT = LINE
```

```
          *
          *   Find occurrences of "T" marking them with @ operator
          *
6         NEXT   LINE BREAK('T') @X 'T' =            :F(PRINT)
          *
          *   Store up underlinings for this line in UNDER
          *
7                UNDER = UNDER DUPL(' ',X) '-'    :(NEXT)
          *
          *   End of line reached - print underlinings
          *
8         PRINT OUTPUT = UNDER
9                UNDER =            :(MORE)
10        END
```

```
STORE USED      1427
STORE LEFT      24250
COMP ERRORS     0
REGENERATIONS   0
COMP TIME-MSEC 110
```

REMEMBER ME WHEN I AM GONE AWAY,

GONE FAR AWAY INTO THE SILENT LAND;
       - -   -
WHEN YOU CAN NO MORE HOLD ME BY THE HAND,
                                -
NOR I HALF TURN TO GO YET TURNING STAY.
       -     -   - -   -
REMEMBER ME WHEN NO MORE DAY BY DAY

YOU TELL ME OF OUR FUTURE THAT YOU PLANNED:
        -           - -
ONLY REMEMBER ME; YOU UNDERSTAND
                        -
IT WILL BE LATE TO COUNSEL THEN OR PRAY.
 -          -   -   -
YET IF YOU SHOULD FORGET ME FOR A WHILE
 -                 -
AND AFTERWARDS REMEMBER, DO NOT GRIEVE:
       -                      -
FOR IF THE DARKNESS AND CORRUPTION LEAVE
        -                       -
A VESTIGE OF THE THOUGHTS THAT ONCE I HAD,
       -     -   -   - -
BETTER BY FAR YOU SHOULD FORGET AND SMILE
 --   -
THAN THAT YOU SHOULD REMEMBER AND BE SAD.
 -     -   -

```
NORMAL END
IN STATEMENT    10
RUN TIME-MSEC   70
STMTS EXECUTED 147
MCSEC / STMT   476
REGENERATIONS   0
```

The cursor position operator is used to mark the position of the first T in LINE. All text up to the character after this T is deleted from LINE and the underlining character (a minus sign) preceded by the appropriate number of spaces is put into UNDER. For the line

```
GONE FAR AWAY INTO THE SILENT LAND
```

after the first time that

```
NEXT   LINE BREAK('T') aX 'T' =         :F(PRINT)
```

is executed LINE contains O THE SILENT LAND and X is 16, indicating that BREAK('T') has moved the cursor to position 16. UNDER then contains 16 spaces followed by -. For the next T, X is 2 and LINE becomes HE SILENT LAND. UNDER now is 16 spaces - 2 spaces -. UNDER is printed when no more T's are found in LINE. It is set to the null string before the next line is dealt with.

7.2
```
         ***********************************************************
         *
         *   Program to print out all the words which have a
         *   doubled letter
         *
         ***********************************************************
         *
         *   Initialisation
         *
1                &ANCHOR = 0
2                &TRIM = 1
3                &STLIMIT = 10000
4                LETTERS = 'ABCDEFGHIJKLMNOPQRSTUVWXYZ'
5                WORDPAT = BREAK(LETTERS) SPAN(LETTERS) . WORD
6                DOUBLE = LEN(1) $ V *V
         *
         *   Read data and look for words with doubled letters
         *
7        READ    LINE = INPUT        :F(END)
8        NEXT    LINE WORDPAT =       :F(READ)
9                WORD DOUBLE          :F(NEXT)
10               OUTPUT = WORD        :(NEXT)
11       END
```

```
STORE USED       1434
STORE LEFT       24243
COMP ERRORS      0
REGENERATIONS    0
COMP TIME-MSEC  130
```

```
TELL
PLANNED
WILL
DARKNESS
CORRUPTION
BETTER
```

```
NORMAL END
IN STATEMENT    11
RUN TIME-MSEC   170
STMTS EXECUTED 264
MCSEC / STMT    643
REGENERATIONS   0
```

7.3

```
         ***********************************************************
         *
         *  This program counts the occurrences of all words
         *  beginning A, E, I, O and U using a table for each vowel
         *
         ***********************************************************
         *
         *  Initialisation
         *
1            &STLIMIT = 10000
2            &ANCHOR = 1
3            &TRIM = 1
4            LETTERS = 'ABCDEFGHIJKLMNOPQRSTUVWXYZ'
5            WORDPAT = BREAK(LETTERS) SPAN(LETTERS) . WORD
6            VOWELS = 'AEIOU'
7            DEFINE('PRINT(WORDS,LET)TEXT,I,J,HEAD')
         *
         *  Construct table names using indirect referencing
         *
8            V = VOWELS
9    CONS    V LEN(1) . CH =                    :F(READ)
10           $CH = TABLE()                       :(CONS)
         *
         *  Read a line
         *
11   READ    LINE = INPUT                        :F(OUT)
         *
         *  Count words
         *
12   NEXT    LINE WORDPAT =                      :F(READ)
13           WORD ANY(VOWELS) . CH               :F(NEXT)
14           ($CH)<WORD> = ($CH)<WORD> + 1       :(NEXT)
         *
         *  Print results
         *  Calling function PRINT for each table
         *
15   OUT     V = VOWELS
16   NEXTV   V LEN(1) . CH =                     :F(END)
17           PRINT($CH,CH)                        :(NEXTV)
         *
         *  Function PRINT(WORDS,LET) prints table WORDS.
         *  LET is a letter used in the headings
         *
18   PRINT    OUTPUT =
```

```
19                    OUTPUT =
20                    HEAD = 'Table of words beginning with letter ' LET
21                    OUTPUT = DUPL(' ',10) HEAD
22                    OUTPUT = DUPL(' ',10) DUPL('-',SIZE(HEAD))
23                    WORDS = CONVERT(WORDS,'ARRAY')          :F(PRINT.4)
24                    I = 1
25          PRINT.1   J = 1
26          PRINT.2   TEXT = TEXT WORDS<I,2> ' ' WORDS<I,1>
            +   DUPL(' ', 14 - SIZE(WORDS<I,1>))           :F(PRINT.3)
27                    I = I + 1
28                    J = LT(J,4) J + 1                      :S(PRINT.2)
29                    OUTPUT = TEXT
30                    TEXT =                                 :(PRINT.1)
31          PRINT.3   OUTPUT = TEXT                          :(RETURN)
            *
            *   Message if no words found
            *
32          PRINT.4   OUTPUT = 'No words beginning with letter ' LET
            +   ' found'          :(RETURN)
33          END


STORE USED      1505
STORE LEFT      24172
COMP ERRORS     0
REGENERATIONS   0
COMP TIME-MSEC  270
```

```
              Table of words beginning with letter A
              ----------------------------------------
4   AND           2   A           2   AWAY          1   AM
1   AFTERWARDS


              Table of words beginning with letter E
              ----------------------------------------
No words beginning with letter E found


              Table of words beginning with letter I
              ----------------------------------------
1   INTO          2   IF          1   IT            3   I


              Table of words beginning with letter O
              ----------------------------------------
1   ONLY          1   OR          1   ONCE          1   OUR
2   OF


              Table of words beginning with letter U
              ----------------------------------------
1   UNDERSTAND
```

```
NORMAL END
IN STATEMENT    33
RUN TIME-MSEC   230
STMTS EXECUTED  408
MCSEC / STMT    563
REGENERATIONS   0
```

8.1

```
        ************************************************************
        *
        *   Program to count the number of people in each occupation
        *   and print out their names and identification numbers
        *
        ************************************************************
        *
        *   Initialisation
        *
1               &ANCHOR  = 1
2               &TRIM = 1
3               &STLIMIT = 10000.
4               SPLIT = LEN(2) . IDEN LEN(18) LEN(1) . JOB
      +   BREAK('*') . NAME
5               DATA('PERSON(COUNT,WHO)')
6               PEOPLE = TABLE()
7               JOBCODES = 'ADJLT'
8               JOBS = TABLE()
9               JOBNAMES = 'Accountant/Doctor/Journalist/Lawyer/'
      +   'Teacher/'
        *
        *   Set up table of abbreviations and jobs
        *
10              J = JOBCODES
11      SETUP   J LEN(1) . CODE =                          :F(MORE)
12              JOBNAMES BREAK('/') . JOBTITLE '/' =    :S(OK)
13              OUTPUT = 'Error - not enough jobs to set up table'
      +   :(END)
14      OK      JOBS<CODE> = JOBTITLE                       :(SETUP)
        *
        *   Read data and load table
        *
15      MORE    LINE = INPUT           :F(PRINT)
16              LINE SPLIT
17              IDENT(PEOPLE<JOB>)     :F(NOTNEW)
        *
        *   Each new table element must be a PERSON
        *
18              PEOPLE<JOB> = PERSON(0)
19      NOTNEW  COUNT(PEOPLE<JOB>) = COUNT(PEOPLE<JOB>) + 1
        *
        *   Names are separated by / in WHO field
        *
```

```
20              WHO(PEOPLE<JOB>) = WHO(PEOPLE<JOB>) ' ' IDEN ' '
     +  NAME '/'      :(MORE)
     *
     *  Print results
     *
21      PRINT  JOBCODES LEN(1) . CODE =                    :F(END)
22             OUTPUT = JOBS<CODE> ' ' COUNT(PEOPLE<CODE>)
23      NEXTP  WHO(PEOPLE<CODE>) BREAK('/') . OUTPUT '/' =
     +  :S(NEXTP)
24             OUTPUT =                                    :(PRINT)
25      END
```

```
STORE USED      1531
STORE LEFT      24146
COMP ERRORS     0
REGENERATIONS   0
COMP TIME-MSEC 230
```

```
Accountant  2
   3 JONES, HENRY
  14 PETERSON, WILLIAM

Doctor  3
   7 WILLIAMS, PETER
   9 HARRIS, GEOFFREY
  11 MILES, JOSEPH

Journalist  3
   5 SCOTT, MICHAEL
   6 JAMES, KEITH
  12 WHITE, PETER

Lawyer  5
   1 SMITH, JOHN
   4 WILSON, DAVID
   8 GREEN, GEORGE
  10 ROBERTS, DAVID
  13 EDWARDS, ALAN

Teacher  1
   2 BROWN, JAMES
```

```
NORMAL END
IN STATEMENT    25
RUN TIME-MSEC   90
STMTS EXECUTED 138
MCSEC / STMT   652
REGENERATIONS   0
```

8.2

```
     ************************************************************
     *
     *   Program to store and print out all lines which end in
     *   Y or D
     *
     ************************************************************
     *
     *   Initialisation
     *
1          &ANCHOR = 1
2          &TRIM = 1
3          &STLIMIT = 10000
4          DATA('LIST(LINE,LINE.NO,NEXT)')
5          DEFINE('PRINT(HEAD,COUNT)I')
6          YD = ANY('YD') . L
7          YDEND = RTAB(1) YD | RTAB(2) YD ANY('.,;:?')
     *
     *   Read data
     *
8   MORE  LINE = INPUT        :F(PRINTIT)
9          LINENO = LINENO + 1
     *
     *   Look for D or Y at end of LINE ignoring punctuation
     *
10         LINE YDEND          :F(MORE)
     *
     *   Count number of lines
     *
11         $(L 'COUNT') = $(L 'COUNT') + 1
     *
     *   Head of list
     *
12         $(L 'HEAD') = EQ($(L 'COUNT'),1) LIST(LINE,LINENO)
    +    :F(ADD)
13         $(L 'CURR') = $(L 'HEAD')            :(MORE)
     *
     *   Subsequent entries
     *
14  ADD   NEXT($(L 'CURR')) = LIST(LINE,LINENO)
15         $(L 'CURR') = NEXT($(L 'CURR'))     :(MORE)
     *
     *   Print lists
     *
16  PRINTIT  PRINT(DHEAD,DCOUNT)
17           PRINT(YHEAD,YCOUNT)                :(END)
     *
     *   Function PRINT(HEAD,COUNT) prints a list of which
     *   HEAD is the head.  COUNT is the number of entries
     *   in the list
     *
18  PRINT   I = HEAD
19  PRINT.1 OUTPUT = DUPL(' ',4 - SIZE(LINE.NO(I))) LINE.NO(I)
    +    ' ' LINE(I)
```

```
20               I = DIFFER(NEXT(I)) NEXT(I)      :S(PRINT.1)
21               OUTPUT = DUPL(' ',45) 'Total: ' COUNT
22               OUTPUT =                         :(RETURN)
23       PRINT.END
24       END
```

```
STORE USED      1750
STORE LEFT      23927
COMP ERRORS     0
REGENERATIONS   0
COMP TIME-MSEC 210
```

```
  2 GONE FAR AWAY INTO THE SILENT LAND;
  3 WHEN YOU CAN NO MORE HOLD ME BY THE HAND,
  6 YOU TELL ME OF OUR FUTURE THAT YOU PLANNED:
  7 ONLY REMEMBER ME; YOU UNDERSTAND
 12 A VESTIGE OF THE THOUGHTS THAT ONCE I HAD,
 14 THAN THAT YOU SHOULD REMEMBER AND BE SAD.
                                           Total: 6


  1 REMEMBER ME WHEN I AM GONE AWAY,
  4 NOR I HALF TURN TO GO YET TURNING STAY.
  5 REMEMBER ME WHEN NO MORE DAY BY DAY
  8 IT WILL BE LATE TO COUNSEL THEN OR PRAY.
                                           Total: 4
```

```
NORMAL END
IN STATEMENT    24
RUN TIME-MSEC   70
STMTS EXECUTED 117
MCSEC / STMT    598
REGENERATIONS   0
```

9.1

```
**************************************************************
*
*    Program to print out the words in alphabetical order
*    together with their frequencies
*
**************************************************************
*
*    Initialisation
*
1        &ANCHOR = 1
2        &TRIM = 1
3        &STLIMIT = 10000
4        LETTERS = 'ABCDEFGHIJKLMNOPQRSTUVWXYZ'
5        WORDPAT = BREAK(LETTERS) SPAN(LETTERS) . WORD
6        LOWERS = 'abcdefghijklmnopqrstuvwxyz'
7        COUNT = TABLE()
*
*    Read data and load words into table COUNT
*
```

```
8        MORE  LINE = INPUT                              :F(PRINT)
9        AGAIN LINE WORDPAT =                            :F(MORE)
10             COUNT<WORD> = COUNT<WORD> + 1    :(AGAIN)
         *
         *   Print words after a heading
         *
11       PRINT HEAD = 'Words in forward alphabetical order'
12             OUTPUT = DUPL(' ',15) HEAD
13             OUTPUT = DUPL(' ',15) DUPL('-',SIZE(HEAD))
14             OUTPUT =
         *
         *   Convert table to an array and sort it
         *
15             COUNT = SORT(CONVERT(COUNT,'ARRAY'))    :F(EMPTY)
16             I = 1
         *
         *   Convert words to upper and lower case
         *
17       NEXTW COUNT<I,1> LEN(1) . C REM . REST        :F(COLS)
18             COUNT<I,1> = C REPLACE(REST,LETTERS,LOWERS)
19             I = I + 1                               :(NEXTW)
         *
20       COLS  VTOT = I - 1
21             NCOL = 4
22             L = VTOT / NCOL + 1
         *
         *   New line for printing
         *
23             NROW = 1
24       SETJ  J = 1
25             I = NROW
26       NEXTR ROW = ROW LPAD(COUNT<I,2>,2) ' ' RPAD(COUNT<I,1>,12)
27             I = LT(I,VTOT) I + L          :F(OP)
28             J = LT(J,NCOL) J + 1          :S(NEXTR)
29       OP    OUTPUT = ROW
30             ROW =
31             NROW = LT(NROW,L) NROW + 1    :S(SETJ)
         *
         *   Last line
         *
32             OUTPUT = ROW                 :(END)
         *
         *   Error message for empty table
         *
33       EMPTY OUTPUT = 'Error - table empty'
34       END
```

```
STORE USED      1488
STORE LEFT      24189
COMP ERRORS     0
REGENERATIONS   0
COMP TIME-MSEC 260
```

```
                    Words in forward alphabetical order
                    ------------------------------------
```

2 A	1 Future	2 No	1 Than
1 Afterwards	1 Go	1 Nor	3 That
1 Am	2 Gone	1 Not	4 The
4 And	1 Grieve	2 Of	1 Then
2 Away	1 Had	1 Once	1 Thoughts
2 Be	1 Half	1 Only	2 To
1 Better	1 Hand	1 Or	1 Turn
3 By	1 Hold	1 Our	1 Turning
1 Can	3 I	1 Planned	1 Understand
1 Corruption	2 If	1 Pray	1 Vestige
1 Counsel	1 Into	5 Remember	3 When
1 Darkness	1 It	1 Sad	1 While
2 Day	1 Land	3 Should	1 Will
1 Do	1 Late	1 Silent	2 Yet
2 Far	1 Leave	1 Smile	7 You
2 For	6 Me	1 Stay	
2 Forget	2 More	1 Tell	

```
NORMAL END
IN STATEMENT     34
RUN TIME-MSEC    380
STMTS EXECUTED  755
MCSEC / STMT     503
```

The columns of words read downwards, but the program can only print across the line. The program must therefore work out the order in which the words are loaded into ROW for printing. The number of rows (L) is the number of different words (VTOT) divided by the number of columns (NCOL) plus 1. I is the subscript to COUNT, starting at 1 for the first word of the first row (the word A). L is added to I to get the position in COUNT of the second word to be printed (here Future). L is added again to I to get the third word (here No) etc. When I is greater than VTOT we need to print ROW, then empty ROW and set I to 2, the starting point in COUNT of the second row.

9.2

```
        ***********************************************************
        *
        *   Program to list the people by place of birth, then
        *   date of birth
        *
        ***********************************************************
        *
        *   Initialisation
        *
1               &STLIMIT = 10000
2               &ANCHOR = 1
3               &TRIM = 1
4               MONTHS = TABLE(12)
5               MONTHS<'01'> = 'January'
```

```
6              MONTHS<'02'> = 'February'
7              MONTHS<'03'> = 'March'
8              MONTHS<'04'> = 'April'
9              MONTHS<'05'> = 'May'
10             MONTHS<'06'> = 'June'
11             MONTHS<'07'> = 'July'
12             MONTHS<'08'> = 'August'
13             MONTHS<'09'> = 'September'
14             MONTHS<'10'> = 'October'
15             MONTHS<'11'> = 'November'
16             MONTHS<'12'> = 'December'
       *
       *   Set up table of places
       *
17             PLACES = TABLE(6)
18             PLACECODES = 'NYLNTOEDCHSY'
19             FULLPLACES = 'New York/London/Toronto/Edinburgh/'
       +  'Chicago/Sydney/'
20     NXTP   PLACECODES LEN(2) . CODE =                    :F(SET)
21             FULLPLACES BREAK('/') . PLACE '/' =          :F(ERR)
22             PLACES<CODE> = PLACE                         :(NXTP)
23     ERR    OUTPUT = 'Error in setting up table of places' :(END)
       *
24     SET    PEOPLE = ARRAY(14)
25             DATA('PERSON(TOWN,BIRTH,IDEN,NAME)')
       *
26             BREAKUP = LEN(2) . NUM LEN(2) . PLACE LEN(8) . DBIRTH
       +  LEN(9) BREAK('*') . PNAME
       *
       *   Read a line
       *
27             I = 1
28     MORE   LINE = INPUT                   :F(SORTS)
       *
       *   Extract fields and load them into PEOPLE
       *   Each element of PEOPLE is a PERSON
       *
29             LINE BREAKUP
30             PEOPLE<I> = PERSON(PLACES<PLACE>,DBIRTH,NUM,PNAME)
31             I = I + 1                       :(MORE)
       *
       *   Sort array on TOWN and then BIRTH
       *
32     SORTS PEOPLE = SORT(SORT(PEOPLE,.BIRTH),.TOWN)
       *
       *   Print array
       *
33             I = 1
34             NEWPLACE = TOWN(PEOPLE<I>)
       *
       *   Only print place if it is different from previous one
       *
35     NEW    OUTPUT =
36             OUTPUT = NEWPLACE
```

```
37       SAME  BIRTH(PEOPLE<I>) LEN(4) . YR LEN(2) . MONTH LEN(2)
         +  . DAY
38            DAY '0' = ' '
39            OUTPUT = DUPL(' ',5)
         +  RPAD(DAY ' ' MONTHS<MONTH> ' ' YR,20)
         +  IDEN(PEOPLE<I>) ' ' NAME(PEOPLE<I>)            :F(END)
40            I = LT(I,14) I + 1                           :F(END)
         *
         *  Check for same place name
         *
41            IDENT(TOWN(PEOPLE<I>),NEWPLACE)              :S(SAME)
42            NEWPLACE = TOWN(PEOPLE<I>)                   :(NEW)
43       END


STORE USED       1656
STORE LEFT       24021
COMP ERRORS      0
REGENERATIONS    0
COMP TIME-MSEC 350


Chicago
      14 November 1898      14   PETERSON, WILLIAM
      31 January 1899        7   WILLIAMS, PETER

Edinburgh
      12 March 1898          5   SCOTT, MICHAEL

London
      21 June 1890           1   SMITH, JOHN
      13 July 1899          11   MILES, JOSEPH
       1 December 1908       4   WILSON, DAVID

New York
      29 July 1888           6   JAMES, KEITH
      16 September 1894      9   HARRIS, GEOFFREY
      15 March 1900          2   BROWN, JAMES
      15 October 1906       13   EDWARDS, ALAN

Sydney
       9 April 1898          3   JONES, HENRY
       4 November 1902       8   GREEN, GEORGE

Toronto
       3 June 1902          12   WHITE, PETER
      29 May 1903           10   ROBERTS, DAVID


NORMAL END
IN STATEMENT    43
RUN TIME-MSEC   130
STMTS EXECUTED 189
MCSEC / STMT    687
REGENERATIONS   0
```

9.3

```
        ************************************************************
        *
        *   Program to change all occurrences of REMEMBER to FORGET
        *   using the anchored mode
        *
        ************************************************************
        *
        *   Initialisation
        *
1             &TRIM = 1
2             &ANCHOR = 1
3             &STLIMIT = 10000
4             PAT = BREAKX('R') . P1 'REMEMBER' REM . P2
        *
        *   Read a line and change all instances of REMEMBER to
        *   FORGET
        *
5   MORE  LINE = INPUT                  :F(END)
6   AGAIN LINE PAT                      :F(PRINT)
7         LINE = P1 'FORGET' P2         :(AGAIN)
        *
        *   Output new version of LINE
        *
8   PRINT OUTPUT = LINE                 :(MORE)
9   END
```

```
STORE USED      1444
STORE LEFT      24233
COMP ERRORS     0
REGENERATIONS   0
COMP TIME-MSEC 100
```

```
FORGET ME WHEN I AM GONE AWAY,
GONE FAR AWAY INTO THE SILENT LAND;
WHEN YOU CAN NO MORE HOLD ME BY THE HAND,
NOR I HALF TURN TO GO YET TURNING STAY.
FORGET ME WHEN NO MORE DAY BY DAY
YOU TELL ME OF OUR FUTURE THAT YOU PLANNED:
ONLY FORGET ME; YOU UNDERSTAND
IT WILL BE LATE TO COUNSEL THEN OR PRAY.
YET IF YOU SHOULD FORGET ME FOR A WHILE
AND AFTERWARDS FORGET, DO NOT GRIEVE:
FOR IF THE DARKNESS AND CORRUPTION LEAVE
A VESTIGE OF THE THOUGHTS THAT ONCE I HAD,
BETTER BY FAR YOU SHOULD FORGET AND SMILE
THAN THAT YOU SHOULD FORGET AND BE SAD.
```

```
NORMAL END
IN STATEMENT    9
RUN TIME-MSEC   30
STMTS EXECUTED 58
MCSEC / STMT   517
REGENERATIONS   0
```

Bibliography

1. R. E. Griswold, J. F. Poage, I. P. Polonsky, *The SNOBOL4 Programming Language*, Second Edition, Englewood Cliffs: Prentice-Hall, 1971.

   The standard reference manual, an essential for serious SNOBOL programming. It is not an easy book for the beginner and many of the examples are from mathematics or computer science.

2. P. R. Newsted, *SNOBOL: An Introduction to Programming*, New Jersey: Hayden Book Company, 1975.

   An introductory book which is easy to understand but can encourage bad programming. It does not say enough about some vital features.

3. R. E. Griswold and M. T. Griswold, *A SNOBOL4 Primer*, Englewood Cliffs: Prentice-Hall, 1973.

   An introductory book which covers the most important aspects of SNOBOL, but the text is not particularly directed at the humanities student.

4. W. D. Maurer, *The Programmer's Introduction to SNOBOL*, Elsevier Computer Science Library, 1976.

   Intended for those who already program in another language rather than for the absolute beginner.

5. L. D. Burnard, 'SNOBOL: The Language for Literary Computing', a series of four articles in *Bulletin of the Association for Literary and Linguistic Computing*, beginning Volume 6, Number 3 (1978), p. 269.

   A witty and well-written series about SNOBOL, giving useful hints on how to get the best from it. The articles assume a knowledge of the syntax of SNOBOL and are not intended for beginners.

6. J. F. Gimpel, *Algorithms in SNOBOL4*, Wiley, 1976.

   Over four hundred pages of SNOBOL functions and explanation, requiring some mathematical knowledge for complete understanding.

7. R. E. Griswold, *String and List Processing in SNOBOL4*, Prentice Hall, 1975.

   Discusses advanced programming techniques in SNOBOL.

Index